Growing Hardy **Orchids**

**Philip Seaton, Phillip Cribb,
Margaret Ramsay & John Haggar**

Contents

Foreword 3

Why grow hardy orchids? 4

Working with nature 6

The orchid family 8

Habitat and ecology 16

Conservation 20

Composts 24

Glasshouse techniques 28

Cultivation in the garden 36

Pests and diseases 44

Raising orchids from seed to flowering plant 50

Dactylorhiza 56

Ophrys 64

Cypripedium 72

Pleione 80

Hardy orchid genera 84

Foreword

The Royal Botanic Gardens, Kew has the oldest collection of cultivated orchids in the world, dating back to the 18 Century. Kew's orchid collection was known to Charles Darwin who was passionate about orchids, especially the UK native species that grew profusely on a bank near his house at Downe in Kent. Kew's contribution to Darwin's orchid studies arose from his close friendship with Joseph Hooker, who became Kew's second director in 1865 upon the death of his father, Sir William Hooker. Both Hookers undoubtedly shared with Darwin their knowledge of the tropical orchid species grown in abundance at Kew. Joseph Hooker established the first full-time post for an orchid specialist at Kew in the 1880s; Kew's incomparable living and preserved orchid collections have attracted eminent scientists and horticulturists ever since.

In the early 1980s, Kew embarked upon The Sainsbury Orchid Conservation Project, orchid growing having been Lady Sainsbury's passion for many years. This project sought to propagate UK native species for reintroduction into the wild at selected sites. Its success led to the publication by Phillip Cribb and Christopher Bailes of *Hardy Orchids* (1983), which provided useful information on basic techniques for growers. Since then, hardy orchids have become more popular with growers, new techniques and composts have been developed, and nursery-raised stock has become widely available, and a more up-to-date account is now needed urgently.

This book is inspired by the earlier popular book *Growing Orchids from Seed*, which describes a viable means of obtaining orchid plants at a time when collecting orchid plants from the wild is actively discouraged and unlawful in many countries. Likewise, the methods outlined in this book on hardy orchid propagation will open new avenues for aficionados of the hardier species. I hope that this well-produced and expertly written book will stimulate growers to take up the cultivation of one of the most fascinating groups of plants on earth.

Professor Stephen Hopper FLS
Director (CEO and Chief Scientist)
Royal Botanic Gardens, Kew

Bletilla striata in the alpine garden at Kew ▶

3

Why grow hardy orchids?

Ophrys tenthredinifera

There is a myth that orchids are too exotic and demanding for all but the most expert gardeners. As a result, hardy orchids are under-utilised in gardens, even though it is possible to raise large numbers of plants from seed and many people would like to grow them. This book shows you how to cultivate hardy orchids in a cool greenhouse or outside, in their rightful place alongside other garden plants.

Orchids from tropical and sub-tropical climates are tender in temperate regions where they generally need a warm greenhouse to survive. Hardy orchids, however, originate from the temperate zones of the world or from the higher mountains of the subtropics. They are much better suited to cooler climates. Although some require a frost-free greenhouse or a cold-frame, many will thrive outside.

It is impossible to cover all of the orchids that have potential as garden plants in a slim volume, instead we provide examples that are relatively easy to grow from seed and are less demanding in cultivation. We are particularly keen to encourage the cultivation of hardy orchid hybrids. These have a number of advantages over their parental species: they are usually easier to grow, they are more tolerant of a greater variety of composts, soils and climates, and they often possess hybrid vigour.

The propagation and cultivation of hardy orchids has a role in conservation. Many hardy orchid species are naturally rare, declining or even endangered and locally extinct. Cultural methods, particularly growing from seed, can be used to eliminate the need to collect orchids from the wild, thereby maintaining natural populations. In some circumstances, plants grown from seed have been used to boost populations that are in serious decline. Even where an orchid species is no longer found in the wild, the re-introduction of plants into suitable habitats, for example, where the species has been collected to extinction, is one strategy that has already been successful.

▼ *Dactylorhiza foliosa* **growing in the Alpine House at Kew**

▼ *Cypripedium* **hybrids in a garden setting**

Working with nature

Cypripedium tibeticum in Yunnan, China

Most orchids grow in precisely defined habitats and are adapted to the environment in which they grow. Understanding where and how an orchid grows in the wild and its natural life cycle enables the grower to follow that natural cycle. This is the secret to successful orchid cultivation. The natural cycle provides practical guidance about when to sow the seeds, how long the seedlings should be rested, and when flask-grown seedlings should be weaned and transplanted into compost.

In northern Europe, Asia and North America and in montane regions, winter temperatures well below freezing are common and the weather is too severe for orchids to grow actively during the winter. In these regions, orchids survive the winter by retreating underground as a rhizome or tuber, allowing the above-ground parts to die down as conditions become harsh. In the spring, fresh, green shoots appear, and the underground food reserves are replenished during the active growth period in the summer.

In Mediterranean regions, the challenge is not so much cold winters as hot, dry summers. Hence, many Mediterranean orchids are "winter green". These plants survive the dry summer months as tubers or swollen roots and have a rosette of leaves that emerges above ground in the autumn. They grow actively during the cool, moist winters and flower in the spring or early summer.

Orchids that grow in more tropical and sub-tropical regions also have a number of adaptations that help them to minimise water loss when growing in dry environments. These include swollen stems (called pseudobulbs), leathery or fleshy leaves (of various shapes from cylindrical to flattened), and stout roots that are covered in several layers of dead cells (called the velamen). Some species that have a degree of hardiness, including some calanthes, cymbidiums and pleiones, also have pseudobulbs.

▼ **A dormant *Pleione* bulb with two flower buds. Pleiones shed their leaves before the onset of winter.**

▼ **A rosette of leaves forms as an *Ophrys* plant emerges in autumn**

▼ **Pseudobulbs of *Cymbidium* retain their leaves throughout the year**

The orchid family

Ophrys mammosa

Anacamptis morio

Epipactis mairei

Himantoglossum hircinum

Cypripedium margaritaceum

Cymbidium goeringii

Calanthe hancockii

The orchid family (Orchidaceae) is extraordinarily diverse and includes about 25,000 species in around 850 genera. Although orchids are predominantly tropical and subtropical, their range extends beyond the Arctic Circle in the north and as far south as Macquarie Island, which lies between Australia and the Antarctic.

Hardy orchids are found in temperate regions around the globe, including Asia, North America, Europe, southern Australia and southern South America, as well as on subtropical mountains. Like lilies, daffodils and tulips, orchids belong to the Monocotyledon grouping of plants, which all have a single seedling leaf.

The distinctive features that separate orchids from plants of other families are illustrated here:

Orchids form a protocorm from which the first root and shoot develop

Orchids have tiny seeds that lack any endosperm and comprise an embryo (stained red) and a seed coat (testa)

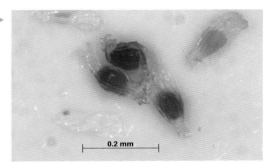

0.2 mm

The male and female organs of orchid flowers are fused into a column, clearly visible in this *Ophrys* flower as the large green structure

An intimate fungal association (mycorrhiza) is necessary to initiate the germination of orchid seeds and sometimes lasts throughout the plant's life

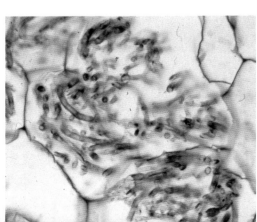

Orchids roots are protected by the velamen. For hardy orchids, this is usually a single layer of dead cells, but for this epiphyte, *Sophronitis cernua*, the white velamen is comprised of several cell layers.

Flowers

It takes at least two years and usually three to five years after germination for orchid plants to reach maturity and flower. Orchid flowers are diverse and complex. They have evolved an astonishing suite of weird and wonderful adaptations that allow them to attract specific pollinators, usually insects, which transfer their pollen masses to the stigma of another flower, thus ensuring cross-fertilisation. Nevertheless, a significant number of species, including our native bee orchid (*Ophrys apifera*), are self-pollinated and produce viable seeds without a pollen vector.

The underlying structure of orchid flowers remains simple, but it is highly modified in comparison with the more typical monocotyledon flower structures of distant relatives such as *Trillium* or *Lilium*. Monocotyledons usually have their floral parts arranged in threes or multiples of three, and orchids are no exception; this can be seen in the two outermost whorls of the flower, which consist of three sepals and three petals. Behind the flower is the ovary, which again is tripartite in many orchids. The ovary contains large numbers, often thousands, of miniscule ovules (eggs), each a potential seed, and only begins to swell and develop once fertilisation has occurred.

In most species, the two lateral petals are uppermost in the flower and differ markedly from the third petal, which lies at the bottom of the flower. The most obvious feature of an orchid flower is the modification of this third petal to become a showy, often brightly coloured lip or labellum. This usually acts as an attraction and landing platform for potential pollinators, which are guided toward the pollen and the stigma surface by its form. In many species, the lip is lobed and extended at the base into a pouch-shaped (saccate) or thread-like (filiform) spur, which may or may not contain nectar. In most orchid flowers, the lip lies uppermost in the flower bud, with the column below, but when the flower opens the ovary twists to present the lip at the bottom of the flower. This twisting is termed resupination.

▲ *Cypripedium* 'Ulla Silkens'

Slipper orchids are trap flowers, and their lip is modified to form a pouch or 'slipper' into which the pollinating insect is lured. *Cypripedium* flowers often assist the pollinator in its scramble for freedom by having a ladder of hairs inside the rear surface of the lip.

Reproductive organs

The reproductive organs at the centre of an orchid flower have many fewer parts than those of most flowers, and the male and female organs are fused into a single structure called the column. In most orchids, a single anther lies at the apex of the column. Orchid pollen is not powdery but is fused into discrete masses called pollinia, of which there are usually two or four (or rarely eight), often concealed in the anther cap at the tip of the column. In some species, the pollinia are attached by a slender stalk to a sticky disc called the viscidium. Slipper orchids differ in having two anthers, one either side of the column, and their pollen masses are sticky.

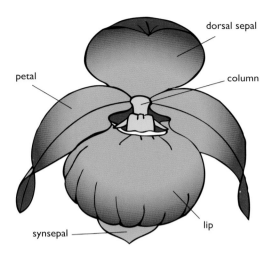

dorsal sepal

petal

column

lip

synsepal

▲ **Cypripedium flower showing the typical pouch or slipper. The two sepals are fused into a synsepal.**

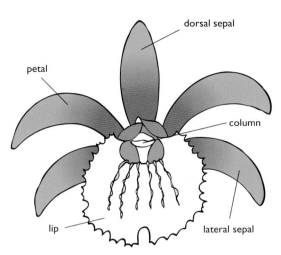

dorsal sepal

petal

column

lip

lateral sepal

▲ **Pleione flower with the column clearly showing in the centre**

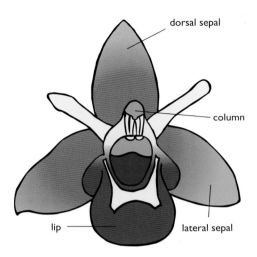

dorsal sepal

column

lip

lateral sepal

▲ **The pollen of a bee orchid (Ophrys apifera) is in two pouches at the apex of the column**

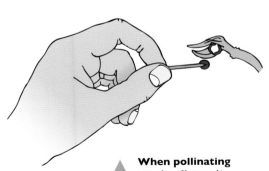

▲ **When pollinating cypripediums, it is often easier to remove the pouch before smearing pollen on the stigma**

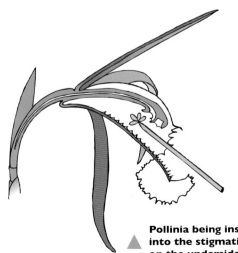

▲ **Pollinia being inserted into the stigmatic cavity on the underside of the column of a Pleione flower**

▲ **Pollination of an Ophrys flower. Pollen should be inserted into the sigma as indicated by the arrow**

The stigma, normally located on the lower surface of the column, is usually a lobed sticky depression situated below and behind the anther. In some terrestrial genera, such as *Habenaria*, the stigmas can have two lobes with the receptive surfaces at the apex of each lobe. In many orchid species, the pollen masses are transferred to the stigmatic surface by a modified lobe of the stigma called the rostellum. This is a projection of various shapes that captures the pollen masses as the pollinator passes beneath on its way out of the flower.

▼ **Bee with pollinia attached to its thorax entering a *Chloraea* flower**

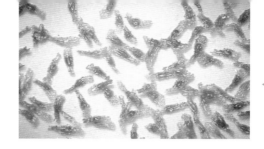

◀ **Orchid seeds are minute and are often produced in their tens of thousands by an individual plant**

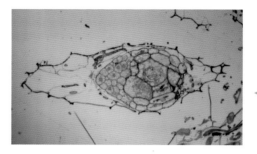

◀ **The seed's embryo and thin seed coat can be seen clearly in section under a microscope (x 300)**

Capsules and seeds

Growers must bear in mind that seed development can take from weeks to several months to complete.

Orchids produce capsules that are usually dry when mature and open along three or six longitudinal slits to release the seeds.

Orchid seeds are very different from those of most flowering plants because they lack a food reserve (endosperm). In fact, orchid seeds are balloon-like, comprising only an embryo (a ball of about one hundred or so cells) and a honeycomb-like seed coat. They have evolved to be dispersed on the merest breath of breeze and are capable of long-distance travel. Thus, orchids have some of the characteristics of weedy plants: they can rapidly colonise newly disturbed land and often turn up unexpectedly on islands or on bare soil.

What orchid seeds lack in size they more than make up for in numbers, with some species producing a million or more seeds per capsule. Because of the miniscule investment needed to produce an individual seed, a single plant of *Dactylorhiza*, for example, releases many thousands of seeds during its lifetime.

Stems and leaves

Orchids vary in size immensely. Many species are small herbaceous plants, but in the tropics, they can form bulky masses that grow on rocks (lithophytes) or on tree trunks or branches (epiphytes). *Vanilla* and *Galeola* orchids are vines that can reach 30 m in length. By contrast, most hardy orchids root in soil and seldom reach 1 m in height, most being 15–100 cm tall.

Because orchids are found in an enormous variety of habitats, their vegetative features are extremely variable. Major adaptations have evolved to combat adverse environmental conditions, in particular the problems of water conservation and marked seasonality.

▶ *Dactylorhiza maculata* seedlings have the sword-shaped leaves that are typical of this genus

Cypripediums have large thin leaves. These plants have been pollinated by hand and have labels to show which crosses have been made. ▶

▶ **Many tropical epiphytic orchids, such as *Vanilla planifolia*, have thick, leathery leaves that allow them to survive dry periods**

13

Germination: dependent on fungi

Orchids have an unusual and rather complex life cycle that sets them apart from most other flowering plants.

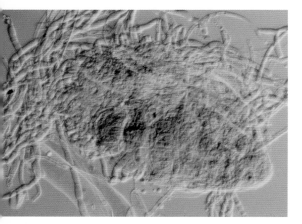

First, orchid seeds are unique in that their seeds must meet a compatible fungal partner (symbiont) in order to germinate.

◀ **Fungal hyphae entering an orchid embryo**

Second, orchids do not produce the single, green, spear-shaped seedling leaf (cotyledon) typical of monocotyledons. Instead, the first structure to develop from an orchid embryo is a top-shaped or more or less cylindrical structure called the protocorm. This structure produces root hairs or rhizoids through which fungal hyphae penetrate to connect the protocorm to the substrate.

A few of the seeds on this medium have germinated to form protocorms

Since the beginning of the 19th century, we have known that the roots of adult orchid plants growing in their natural habitats have fungi that grow within their root tissue. The fungal associations were later named mycorrhiza (from the Latin *myco* (fungus) and *rhiza* (root)). Many plant species form mycorrhiza, which mostly help them in taking up phosphates from the soil, but the lack of a food reserve that is unique to orchid seeds means that orchid protocorms are also initially totally dependent on their fungal partner as a source of carbon.

In most orchids, the first leaf emerges from the protocorm and the first root follows. Most orchids then begin to photosynthesise and the role of the fungal partner as a nutrient source diminishes as the seedling grows. The extent to which orchids continue to depend on mycorrhizal fungi throughout their lifecycle varies between species. A few orchids, such as bird's nest orchid (*Neottia nidus-avis* and the elusive British ghost orchid (*Epipogium aphyllum*), do not photosynthesise at all and are completely dependent on saprophytic fungi for all of their carbon. Other orchids are associated with different fungal symbionts at different stages of their life cycle.

It was not until the end of the 19th century that the French botanist Noël Bernard discovered that orchid seeds germinate only when a compatible fungus is present in the substrate. In the fullness of time, his ground-breaking research allowed growers to germinate many terrestrial orchids symbiotically in cultivation by introducing compatible fungi.

Fortunately for orchid growers, many species can be germinated asymbiotically in cultivation on a simple sterile medium, which provides necessary nutrients, without the need for an associated fungus. Indeed, to date many orchids can only be germinated asymbiotically in cultivation; these include *Orchis* species, *Neotinea*, and most *Cypripedium* and *Ophrys* species.

The bird's nest orchid, *Neottia nidus-avis*, does not photosynthesise and is entirely dependent on its fungal partner for carbon

Temperature and germination

Cold (vernalisation) periods are necessary for the seed germination of some *Dactylorhiza* species (and indeed to stimulate the growth of some already-germinated protocorms). Other species will germinate but then die if the temperature is not low enough. Good cases in point are Mediterranean montane species such as *Orchis anatolica*, *O. quadripunctata*, *O. pauciflora* and *Dactylorhiza romana*, the protocorms of which will only grow well in temperatures of 10–12 °C (50–54 °F). High temperatures often induce death or early dormancy in such species. Even northern *Dactylorhiza* species grow much better at 15 °C (59 °F) than at 21 °C (70 °F).

Seed care for successful germination

Seed storage

As seed of many desirable species is difficult to obtain, it is worth investing a little time and effort in storing it correctly. When kept dry and at refrigerator temperatures (around 5 °C/41 °F), the mature seed of many species can remain viable for a number of years. The key word is dry. Although silica gel can be used as a desiccant, it can reduce seed moisture contents to levels that are too low for optimum storage. A useful alternative is to use dry rice. Any shop-bought rice is suitable, and it can be dried by placing it in a thin layer on a baking tray in an oven at 100 °C (212 °F) and heating until it is slightly toasted. The dried rice should then be placed in a sealed jar while still warm and allowed to cool down before use.

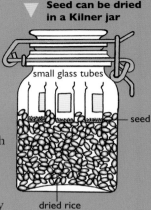

Seed can be dried in a Kilner jar

small glass tubes

seed

dried rice

Seed can be dried for a few days at room temperature (20 °C/68 °F) before being placed in a sealed tube in the refrigerator.

Seeds stored in a refrigerator

Orchid seed in the post

If sending seed through the post, it should be placed in crush-proof packaging such as a padded envelope, otherwise it could be damaged by machinery at the post office. Seed should be sent either in a small strong glass vessel or in a paper packet, not in a plastic bag or tube because it will stick to the walls of these containers.

Pleione formosana

In the wild, most orchids have rather specific habitat and climatic preferences, being sensitive to temperature, rainfall, aspect, shade, soil pH, soil chemistry and soil structure. It is possible that some of these sensitivities reflect the requirements of the fungal partners as much as those of the orchids themselves.

Soil and substrate

Most hardy orchids grow in well-drained soils or substrates where water cannot stagnate around the roots. The majority of European orchids grow in calcareous substrates on chalk, limestone and sand or in fens and marshes. The pH of these soils is alkaline and they are high in calcium ions. By contrast, most Australian and South American terrestrial orchids prefer acidic nutrient-poor soils and will die rapidly if grown in the alkaline soils in which European species thrive. A number of northern-hemisphere species, such as *Cypripedium acaule* and *Dactylorhiza maculata*, are also calcifuges.

Few orchids grow in waterlogged conditions, most preferring free-draining situations. A few species, such as the fen orchid, *Liparis loeselii*, and the North American *Spiranthes cernua* grow with their feet in water; but the roots or pseudobulbs of orchids that grow in boggy or marginal areas are usually clear of the zone of permanent saturation. Other orchids, such as *Calypso bulbosa* and *Hammarbya paludosa*, the bog orchid, grow in sphagnum tufts or cushions in bogs or marshes. Thus, attention to drainage and care with watering are crucial to the cultivation of hardy orchids, and growers must follow the natural seasonality of the plant.

Anacamptis morio **growing in a meadow with a limestone soil** ▶

Cypripedium acaule **from North** ▼
America grows in acidic pine duff

▲
Ophrys lutea **growing on limestone in Spain**

▲
Calypso bulbosa **var.** *speciosa* **growing in a sphagnum bog**

Photo Bernd Haynold

Climate

Temperature and rainfall levels are both critical for orchid growth. Most hardy orchids grow in one of two rainfall regimes: a cold winter and a warm, rather wet summer or a warmer, wetter winter and a dry, hot summer. In the former, winter temperatures can fall well below 0 °C (32 °F), and summer ones seldom rise above 25 °C (77 °F). In the latter, winter temperatures seldom fall below 5 °C (41 °F) and summer temperatures often rise to 30 °C (86 °F) or more. This is reflected in the growth patterns of the orchid species of these two regions: in the former tubers tend to sprout in the spring, grow until summer and flower when the foliage is mature. In the latter, growth occurs throughout the winter months and flowering occurs in the spring as the leaves senesce.

Cephalanthera longifolia, a woodland species ▶

◀ **Cypripedium kentuckiense**

Shade and aspect

Many woodland orchids grow in shaded conditions where direct sunlight is either absent or reduced to only an hour or two a day. Some orchids, for example *Calanthe* species, are particularly sensitive to direct sunlight and thrive in deep shade. For these species, sunlight induces chlorosis, a yellowing of the foliage, and often a lingering death.

Species of *Bletilla*, *Calanthe*, *Cypripedium* or *Spiranthes* can do well in shaded gardens.

Competition

In the wild, most terrestrial orchids are intolerant of competition from other plants, particularly rapidly growing lush vegetation. Thus, at least when establishing themselves, orchids tend to grow in soils that are either somewhat toxic to other plants or devoid of them. Many orchids are pioneer plants of bare soil. Orchids, together with ferns, were the first colonisers of Krakatoa when it re-emerged from the sea after the devastating explosion of the old island in the late 19th century, their light seeds and spores blowing across from the mainland.

The weedy habit of some species is well known. *Ophrys apifera* (bee orchid) and *Anacamptis pyramidalis* are often primary colonisers of bare soil on spoil heaps and road sides, eventually dying out as the surrounding vegetation closes in around them. In calcareous grassland, plants can survive in a closed turf but will not regenerate unless there are bare patches of soil that are relatively free of grass and other herbs, such as rabbit scratchings or where the turf has been broken up by the feet of cattle or other large grazing animals. Lack of competition in cultivation can allow some hardy orchid species to grow better in a pot or garden than in the wild.

Anacamptis pyramidalis often colonises bare soil and struggles to regenerate when there is competition from other plants ▶

Cypripedium calceolus growing in open woodland ▶

▼ *Dactylorhiza sambucina* **in grassland**

Conservation

Cypripedium calceolus

Orchids under threat

A significant number of hardy orchids are threatened with extinction in the wild. Many more are threatened locally or nationally in their natural environments.

Loss and fragmentation of habitat continue to have a significant impact on orchid species around the globe, but orchids also face a number of more subtle threats. What might appear to be very small changes to habitats, such as the modification of mowing or grazing regimes or the addition of fertilisers, have the potential to affect orchid populations dramatically. In general, collection is perhaps a lesser threat to hardy orchids, but it is an important cause of decline for certain groups. In Mediterranean countries such as Turkey and Syria, for example, tuberous orchids are at risk because of the collection of tubers from the wild for the production of 'salep', a nutritious drink (sometimes available as ice-cream) that allegedly has medicinal and aphrodisiac properties. It can take 1,000−4,000 tubers of *Orchis* and *Anacamptis* species to make 1 kg of salep.

The revival of collector interest has led to a resurgence of trade in wild-collected species. Orchids of the showy genus *Cypripedium*, which has a circumboreal distribution with its centre

Cypripedium macranthos plants being raised under shade-cloth in China

of diversity in China, are still collected from the wild in quantity. Although the scale of this trade is difficult to assess, there are clear indications that *Cypripedium* species could become quickly depleted in the wild. There could well be nurseries that are still selling wild-collected plants and it is important that buyers should ask how plants are sourced before making a purchase.

Lady's slipper orchid

Perhaps the best-known example of a nationally threatened plant is *Cypripedium calceolus*, the lady's slipper orchid. For many years, this was one of the UK's rarest plants. The only known wild specimen in Britain, identified in the 1930s almost 20 years after the species was thought extinct in the UK, was guarded around the clock by volunteers. The reintroduction project began in the mid-1990s, when seeds taken from this last wild UK plant were successfully propagated at the Royal Botanic Gardens, Kew. Some of the plants that were subsequently reintroduced into suitable habitats in the UK have now flowered and formed seed capsules in the wild after natural pollination by insects. Fortunately, lady's slipper orchid is still found elsewhere in Europe and northern Asia.

Micropropagated Cypripedium calceolus at Kew ▶

Legal protection

Many orchids are protected under local, national or international legislation. Local by-laws often prevent the removal of plants, for example, from private land or nature reserves. In many countries, especially where particular orchid species are endangered or threatened, national legislation expressly forbids the removal of orchids from both public and private land.

A number of rare species are protected under regulations such as the European Union (EU)'s Habitats Directive, which covers many European orchid species. Each EU member country enacts its own legislation to implement the directive: in the UK, the relevant legislation is the *Wildlife and Countryside Act* of 1981, which has subsequently been updated several times. The *Convention on International Trade in Endangered Species of Fauna and Flora* (CITES) regulates international trade in rare species and bans it for those species listed in Appendix 1 of the convention. All hardy orchids are listed in Appendix 2 of CITES: consequently, valid export and import permits are required for their introduction into the EU from countries outside the EU. Elsewhere, an import permit alone may suffice, depending upon national legislation.

Possible solutions

How can a love of plants and their conservation be reconciled with the desire to grow orchids, which historically has encouraged the over-collection of those very species? Part of the answer is the artificial propagation of plants: it is possible to grow and appreciate hardy orchids without the need to remove plants from the wild.

Plants that are propagated artificially, particularly from seed, are increasingly widely obtainable. They not only have the potential to reduce wild-collection but also often have the advantage of being more vigorous and more easily established in gardens than wild-collected specimens. The challenge now is to concentrate on the propagation of the rarest plants from legal stock to provide plants for the horticultural trade and for conservation purposes.

Orchid societies

Orchid societies can play an important role in conservation, not only by sharing knowledge of orchids and their propagation and cultivation but also by raising awareness of the threats to orchid diversity and reinforcing best practice. They may also be directly involved in conservation projects. The UK's Hardy Orchid Society, for example, prioritises conservation projects such as growing native orchid species from seed, rescuing and transplanting orchids that are threatened by building development, and maintaining an orchid seed bank. This society also advises landowners on how to care for orchids that are growing on their land and has a conservation code that encourages propagation from legitimately acquired material.

Ophrys sphegodes (early spider orchid) is classified as "nationally scarce" in the UK

Photo Ferran Pestaña

Heritage Orchids' show stand promoting the UK Hardy Orchids Society

Buying plants

Hardy orchid plants are increasingly available from specialist growers and alpine plant nurseries. They are usually sold at flowering size, in bud, in leaf or in flower. Most hardy orchids are sold in small pots but species of a few genera, especially cymbidiums, are sold bare-rooted. We recommend that you buy nursery-raised plants, which are almost always in better health and more vigorous than wild-collected ones. Many nurseries are proud of their conservation-friendly credentials and make a feature of their plants being seed-raised or vegetatively propagated. Hybrid plants are almost always nursery-raised and more vigorous than their parental species.

Avoid plants with damaged stems, pseudobulbs, tubers, rhizomes or foliage. Damage can suggest that the plants are wild-collected but, equally, it might indicate that they are diseased. Foliage and flowers should be inspected for signs of viral, bacterial or fungal infection. Shun plants with leaves showing yellow streaks or marks, which are often a sign of viral infection. Black or brown rings often indicate bacterial or fungal infections that can be difficult to eradicate. Burnt leaf-tips might indicate infection or nutrient deficiencies, both good reasons to reject plants.

A number of reputable nurseries display and sell hardy orchids at orchid, alpine garden and general flower shows, and it is possible to buy plants on the internet from an increasing number of nurseries. Unfortunately, dealers in wild-collected plants almost exclusively use the internet. It is best to avoid dealers in the country of origin offering rare species that are not usually found in cultivation, especially recently discovered species, unless you are sure that they have been acquired and propagated legally. If sent without valid CITES documentation, plants are likely to be confiscated and the recipient fined.

Increasingly, seedlings can be bought in flasks. The advantage of buying flasked seedlings is one of price, a flask containing ten or twelve seedlings being no more expensive than a flowering-sized plant. The purchase of flasked seedlings also provides comfort in the certainty that your plants have been nursery-raised. Flasked hardy orchid seedlings do not need CITES certification when imported but might need a phytosanitary certificate.

Pleione hybrids at Ian Butterfield's nursery ▶

Composts

Orchids can be grown in a variety of composts, but commercial composts are designed for leafy, fast-growing plants and don't really suit orchids' requirements. Most growers refine their own composts over time by trial and error.

Basic ingredients

1. **Loam** John Innes Compost no. 2 is suitable for most northern hemisphere hardy orchids. Its chief advantage is that it is sterile. Alternatively, the fine soil from mole hills in alluvial meadows, chalk downs or limestone areas suits many orchids.

2. **Fir bark** is available commercially from many orchid nurseries and on the internet in fine, medium and coarse grades. A fine-grade bark, with particles of about 8 mm (3/8"), works best for most mixes. The bark should be free of any chemical treatment and washed free of dust, which tends to settle at the base of pots blocking the drainage holes. Composted bark can be used as a peat alternative.

3. **Sphagnum** moss absorbs and retains a lot of moisture. It is usually sold in dry blocks, imported from New Zealand or Chile, that expand considerably when water is added.

4. **Horticultural grit, sand or fine quartz** with a particle size of about 5 mm (1/4") opens up a compost and can also be used at the base of a pot or cold frame to provide excellent drainage. Many orchids grow well in sand-based composts, which have good drainage. Sand that is not of horticultural grade can have a high lime content that is not suitable for acid-loving orchids.

5. **Moss peat** Some orchids grow best in a peat-based compost. Moss peat is organic, comparatively uniform, and well aerated. It breaks down slowly and retains water and nutrients. Alternatives to peat, such as coir, are not very good for hardy orchids, and sedge-peat should be avoided.

6. **Charcoal** keeps the compost 'sweet' by adsorbing harmful breakdown products.

7. **Perlite** is an amorphous volcanic glass that retains moisture and an open soil texture. Fine-grade perlite is commercially available from most garden centres and nurseries. It should be washed before use to remove the dust, which can be harmful if inhaled.

8. **Pumice** is a solidified frothy lava, typically created when super-heated, highly pressurised rock is violently ejected from a volcano. It holds water yet improves drainage and can be added to composts for orchids that have a vigourous root system, such as *Cymbidium* species. Pumice is sold commercially under the trade-name Bims®; some brands of non-clumping cat litter (e.g. Sophisticat®) can be used as an alternative.

9. **Fired clay pellets** Commercially available fired-clay products, such as Seramis® clay granules, are water-retentive and can be incorporated to maintain an open compost for finer-rooted orchids.

10. **Vermiculite** is a mica product that is widely available commercially. It is used to improve water retention, aeration and nutrient retention.

11. **Leaf mould** is an ideal alternative to peat. Finely cut beech or oak leaves are gathered while slightly moist and placed in a fastened black polythene bag with a few holes in it. After 1–2 years, the leaves should break down readily and can be rubbed through a garden sieve (about 7 mm (3/8")). The leaves of horse-chestnut, sycamore and evergreen plants should be avoided.

12. **Conifer leaf duff** fallen larch, pine or spruce leaves can be collected and used as a mulch on top of the compost.

Compost mixes and fertilisers

Compost A: European winter-green species

Most species will do well in woodland loam collected from an area with hard limestone bedrock. Alternatively, chalky mole hills with added leaf mould (dry rather than well-rotted) and a little sandy grit produces good results. In both cases, the compost must be allowed to drain freely.

Mixtures to try include:

- 2 parts calcareous or neutral loam, 3 parts beech leaf mould, 2 parts medium sharp grit, 3 parts coarse sharp sand, 1 part crushed shell or limestone grit, and 1 part perlite. In addition, some growers recommend blood, fish- or bonemeal at 12 teaspoons per 50 litres (13 US gallons).

- Alternative composts must be used for plants that prefer neutral or acidic soils, such as some *Dactylorhiza* species. Suitable mixes for calcifuges can be prepared by substituting a more acidic loam, by avoiding lime or limestone and by substituting some of the leaf mould with conifer duff. The following mix has been used successfully:

  1 part acidic loam, 1 part fine bark, 3 parts fine grit, 5 parts pine duff, 1 part coarse Perlite, 2 parts coarse grit, 2 parts sand and 1 part peat.

Compost B: Eurasian winter-dormant tuberous species

Most like well-drained but water-retentive compost with a relatively high organic matter content. Mixtures to try include:

- 3 parts fibrous loam, 2 parts composted bark, 2 parts coarse perlite, 4 parts pine duff or coir, and 4–5 parts coarse grit.

- 3 parts milled peat, 1 part loam, 1 part grit, and 2 parts sharp sand.

- 3 parts fibrous loam, 4 parts pine duff or coir fibre, 2 parts composted bark, 3–5 parts coarse grit, and 2 parts perlite.

- 6 parts Seramis®, 5 parts coarse perlite, 5 parts vermiculite, 1 part loam, and 1 part fine orchid bark. This compost has a low organic matter content and will require very frequent fertiliser use to ensure good growth.

Compost C: *Cypripedium, Epipactis* and *Cephalanthera*

For mature plants and as composts for planting out try:

- 2 parts washed fine bark, 1 part washed horticultural grit and 1 part perlite. Fertilise with liquid feed, e.g. Tomorite, at half strength or with slow-release fertiliser pellets.

- 4 parts pine duff, 1–2 parts neutral loam, composted pine bark or fine moss peat, 1–2 parts fine pine bark, 4–5 parts sharp grit, 1–3 parts sharp sand, and 1 part coarse perlite.

- Coarse-grade pumice as the base; cover roots with a compost of fine-grade pumice or fine propagting sand.

Compost D: Asian hardy orchids such as *Bletilla, Calanthe* and *Cymbidium*

- 9 parts peat, 9 parts fine bark (propagating grade), 1 part perlite, and 1 part leaf mould. Add Vitax or blood, fish- or bonemeal to top fertilise.

Compost E: *Pleione*

- 3 parts fine bark and 2 parts chopped sphagnum. Put compost in the bottom of a tray, place bulbs whose roots have not yet appeared on a layer of chopped sphagnum and fill with compost.

Compost F: Australian hardy orchids

For a basic mix we recommend:

- 2 parts coarse lime-free sand or fine gravel, 1 part rich loam, 1 part fine bark, 1 part leaf mould. Blood and bone 1 dessert spoonful per 9 litres (2.4 US gallons) bucket of mix. The pH of the mix should be between 4.5 and 6, preferably 5, except for species from limestone areas for which a pH of 7 is suitable. Garden lime or dolomite at 1 dessert spoonful per 9 litre bucket of mix can be used to raise the pH if the mixture is too acidic. Plant tubers 3 cm deep (1 1/4") in the compost and cover the compost after filling the pot with chopped pine, larch or spruce needles, which deter slugs and snails. Pots need good ventilation and appropriate light levels: bright light for species from grassland and open areas, shade for woodland species.

Compost G: *Disa, Calypso, Arethusa* and *Calopogon*

- Live sphagnum moss.

Compost H: Epiphytes and lithophytes, e.g. *Dendrobium* and *Neofinetia*

- 9 parts pumice or bark, 1 part chopped New Zealand sphagnum moss, and charcoal pieces.

Compost I: South American terrestrials, e.g. *Chloraea*

We recommend a compost with a minimum of organic material:

- 3 parts perlite, 3 parts Seramis®, 3 parts lava grit, and 1 part fine-grade bark. A minimum temperature of 3 °C (37 °F) is recommended.

Glasshouse techniques

Pleione Bonobo

Vegetative propagation

The underground rhizomes of orchids such as *Cypripedium* and some *Epipactis* often produce more than one growing bud, and under favourable conditions, more than one aerial shoot breaks ground. If planted out, these rhizomes can spread to form large colonies. Clumps can be broken up so long as each offset retains several roots and shoots. When grown in pots, these plants will sometime divide spontaneously. *Epipactis gigantea* is particularly vigorous, and new shoots of this plant may protrude through the bottom of the pot. One technique that has been used successfully is to expose the rhizome by clearing away the soil and to sever it in two with a sterile blade. The soil is then replaced. The severed rhizome should be left until the shoot has died down before being removed and re-potted.

For tuberous orchids, such as *Ophrys*, *Orchis* and *Serapias*, the production of additional (small) tubers is encouraged by growing the plants in a gritty compost mix. Newly formed tubers of *Ophrys* species can be pinched off and potted up in late winter or early spring, before the leaves start to die down. If kept cool and moist, the plants will produce an additional tuber before summer dormancy. Remove the new tubers of *Orchis* and some *Serapias* species while the plant is in flower using a sterile sharp blade. *Dactylorhiza* are summer-green orchids and their new tubers can be twisted off while the plant is in full growth, just after flowering. *Serapias lingua* and *S. olbia* are stoloniferous and naturally produce additional tubers.

Safety note

Scalpel blades should always be treated with care, as they are extremely sharp and potentially dangerous. If you don't have a dedicated 'sharps bin' always wrap blades securely in suitable material before disposing of them in an appropriate bin.

Pleione orchids readily propagate vegetatively, increasing 3- or 4-fold from mature pseudobulbs. Small bulbils can also be produced at the apex of the old pseudobulb. Grow the bulbils in trays or shallow pots on the surface of fine compost and water sparingly until leaves form. It takes 2 to 3 years for these plants to reach flowering size.

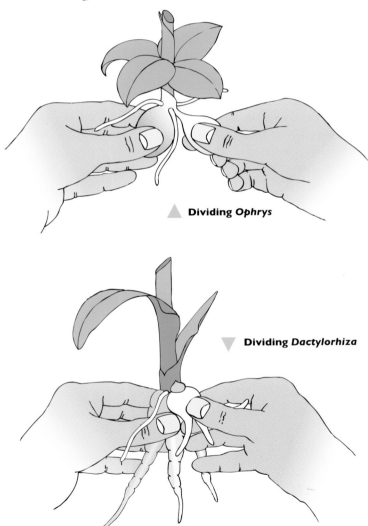

▲ **Dividing *Ophrys***

▼ **Dividing *Dactylorhiza***

29

Growing on flask-raised seedlings

Theoretically, the best time to de-flask and pot up orchids that have been bought or raised as flasked seedlings is just as they are about to leave dormancy and come into new growth. Summer-green species should therefore be potted up in early spring and winter-green species in late autumn. Evergreen orchids should generally be potted up in the spring when increasing light levels will encourage new growth. Select and prepare the compost ahead of de-flasking.

Summer-green species

Summer-green species such as *Dactylorhiza* and *Cypripedium* naturally become dormant in the winter to avoid the freezing conditions that limit moisture availability. These species will benefit from cold winter conditions and can be grown outside or in cold frames.

In autumn, flasked cultures containing plants that are large enough to pot up should be placed in the refrigerator (0−4 °C/32−39 °F) to vernalise for 3−6 months before being potted up. *Cypripedium* species are probably best vernalised in plastic bags or on damp perlite rather than on culture medium: the survival rate of

Ophrys **tubers can be clearly seen in the bottom of the flask**

Summer-green species such as these *Dactylorhiza* seedlings should be de-flasked after vernalisation in the late winter or early spring

dormant plants on media tends to be poor at this stage. It should be noted that the root growth of *Cypripedium* species starts early in the year. Summer-greens should be weaned in the late winter or early spring when outdoor temperatures are likely to be only a few degrees warmer than those in the refrigerator from which they have just emerged. Nutrient agar should be removed because it encourages the growth of bacteria that can kill the plants. Plants can be rinsed free of medium in a bowl of water or under a running cold tap (there is no need to use tepid water if the plants have just emerged from the refrigerator). The fragile seedlings should be handled gently and should not be placed in full sun or allowed to dry out between washing and planting. The tubers or rhizomes should be buried in moist compost. The top 2-3 cm (1") or so of the compost can be seeded with some symbiotic fungus if an appropriate culture is available. Around 12−15 seedlings can be planted in an 11 cm (4") clay pot. The compost should be thoroughly soaked by immersing the pot up to its rim in water. After de-flasking, the pots can be sunk into a plunge bed outside or under a greenhouse bench (as long as they do not get too hot too early in the year).

Winter-green species

Winter-green orchids, including *Ophrys*, *Orchis* and *Serapias*, often grow in the Mediterranean, where their dormancy coincides with hot, dry conditions. For winter growth, they require a frost-free environment, such as a cool glasshouse, cloche or polytunnel, and protection from excessive rain. Avoid over-watering in cold conditions. Mirrors can be used to maximise winter light levels.

Once they have formed leaves and short roots, symbiotically grown winter-green seedlings can be weaned from flasks in the late autumn, but asymbiotic seedlings of European winter-greens require a different strategy. Asymbiotic seedlings cannot be successfully grown out of the flask until they have formed tubers *in vitro*. If grown correctly, the little tubers will form in the spring and early summer. Unfortunately, the first-year dormant tubers

of the majority of asymbiotically grown winter-green European terrestrial orchids do not fare well if left over the warm summer months on agar and a high percentage of them will die. This means that they cannot be deflasked in the autumn. The first year tubers are best potted up in the early summer just as the foliage dies and they begin to turn brown.

Alternatively, winter-green species can be weaned in the late spring while still in leaf so long as a good tuber is already well-formed − the foliage will then die-down after potting up. The little tubers can be protected from desiccation by enclosing the entire pot in a sealed plastic bag and storing it in a dark place until the autumn. A little water can be added back to the pot if it has become too dry.

 Plunged pots of newly weaned symbiotically grown winter-green seedlings in November

Winter-green *Ophrys apifera* seedlings ready to de-flask in late autumn

Pots and pans

Both clay (terracota) and plastic pots or trays may can used, but they require different watering regimes. Clay pots help to maintain a stable environment as they are porous, retaining moisture in the pot itself and help to keep the roots cool, this being especially useful for the coolest-growing species. We recommend using clay pots plunged in a bed of sand for most hardy orchids.

Plastic pots retain more water in the compost and so need less frequent watering. To ensure that they drain well, cut out extra holes around the base. Plastic pots can provide an advantage when using loam-based composts because frequent watering and drying out can cause the formation of a hard impermeable layer. A mulch of fresh pine needles on top of the pots can reduce the need for frequent watering.

Watering

The water requirements of individual plants depend on their origin, plant size, container size, type of compost used and environmental conditions. To find out if a pot needs watering, insert your little finger into the soil surface. If it is cold and damp, the plant does not need additional water. If it is dry on top, it may still be damp below the surface. The weight of the pot gives an indication of the compost's moisture content as it will be lighter if dry. In soft-water areas, tap water can be used for watering, but rainwater or reverse-osmosis water is recommended in areas that have hard water.

For newly potted summer-green seedlings in the spring or newly awakening winter-green tubers in the autumn that have visible

▼ *Cypripedium* **in a plastic half pot**

plant on a mound of compost so that the roots point gently downwards then fill in around the plant

sharp grit or similar to prevent rotting of crown

compost

plastic pot

extra drainage material, e.g. coarse gravel

broken crocks covering drainage holes

▼ *Dactylorhiza* **tuber in a terracota pot**

sharp grit

root

tuber

terracota pot

wire mesh to prevent entry of slugs

shoots but have not yet formed leaves, use a watering can or lance with the rose turned upside down to simulate a soft sprinkling of rain. As the plants develop, water in the mornings on warm days only and avoid getting water into the plants' crowns as they can rot. Water droplets on the leaves magnify sunlight and cause scorching, especially when growing under glass. Therefore, a lance without a rose should be used to water around the plants. As the weather gets warmer, pots should be checked several times a week to ensure adequate watering. Cooler-growing, winter-dormant species need to be kept moist all the year round.

Avoid watering winter-green plants on winter days when the temperature is below 8 °C (46 °F), and avoid leaving any moisture on the leaves overnight at this time. Mediterranean species can be stood in trays of water in spring and early summer but watering should be reduced after flowering or the dormant, drought-resistant tubers will rot.

Place species that are weaned in spring in the shade under the greenhouse bench. Under-bench misting can be used to avoid a sudden drop in humidity during the transition from flask to greenhouse conditions. Temperature and humidity can be kept more stable by plunging the pots into a sand bed and watering the sand. Some growers use a sand bed under a potting bench with fans to increase ventilation and keep the plants cool. Although ventilation reduces humidity and can increase water loss through the leaves, air movement is important to prevent the growth of undesirable fungi and bacteria, which can damage or kill the plantlets. Orchids such as *Dactylorhiza* can be potted up as the new shoot is forming. These plants can be kept on the open bench as long as the temperature does not fluctuate too much and as long as the compost remains damp.

▼ *Ophrys* growing in a plastic pot

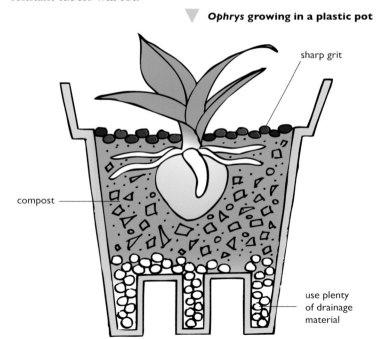

sharp grit

compost

use plenty of drainage material

▼ *Ophrys* in a plunge bed

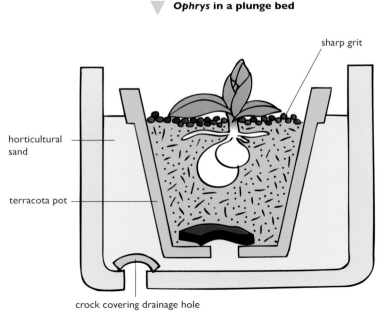

sharp grit

horticultural sand

terracota pot

crock covering drainage hole

Re-potting *Cypripedium*

1. Knock plant out of old pot and remove old compost.

2. Clean dead leaves and roots and wash the plant thoroughly.

3. Take a clean new pot and fill it to about half way with coarse-grade pumice. Place the plant on the pumice and add more to cover the roots.

4. Add composted wood or bark with quartz gravel and perlite to cover all except the shoots. Cover the shoot with a mound of coarse perlite.

5. Fill pot to the brim with the composted wood or bark and quartz gravel and perlite mix.

6. Water well. Pine duff can be added to cover the surface to deter slugs and snails.

Fertilisers and re-potting

Deciduous orchids only need to be fed during their active growth phase and should not be fed when dormant. Evergreen species can be fed throughout the year. The potting compost in which the plants are rooted provides nutrients, sometimes with the help of symbiotic fungi. Unsterilised compost with a high proportion of organic materials will support the growth of the orchids and their symbiotic fungi. Inorganic fertilisers may harm the symbiotic fungi, but watering the compost directly with dilute fish emulsion or seaweed extract is beneficial to the growth of summer-green orchids. A liquid manure, such as dilute (2 ml per litre) Maxicrop® solution can be applied as a foliar feed after alternate waterings, but foliar feeding of winter-green orchids is best avoided during the cold winter months.

Regular re-potting is necessary to replenish nutrients and maintain the structure of the compost. Mediterranean species need to be re-potted annually as they dry out in the summer and the compost becomes dust-like. Re-pot winter-dormant species in the spring and summer-dormant species in the autumn to coincide with the start of new growth. Add 'hoof and horn' to the compost for larger plants but not for newly deflasked seedlings as it can be toxic to them. For symbiotically grown plants, transfer about a third of the old compost to the new pot to ensure that the fungus is carried over. Plants adapt to their position and should be returned to the same place after re-potting.

Summer-green species can be split and re-potted from late summer onwards, the plants often surviving their winter dormancy better in fresh compost. Many species (e.g. *Dactylorhiza* species) establish new roots during the warmer parts of the winter and it is very easy to damage new shoots and roots by re-potting them in the spring. Other orchids do not need re-potting every year and for some genera, such as *Cypripedium*, this practice can be positively harmful.

Traditional clay or plastic pots?

This is a matter of personal preference. Plastic pots retain more moisture, but clay pots 'breathe' more. Even temperatures and moisture levels are best maintained using clay pots plunged in damp sand. Plastic pots are more liable to dry out prematurely when used in such a situation. Place plenty of drainage material in the bottom of the pot. It is also a good idea to place a piece of net over the drainage holes to prevent entry of slugs.

Re-potting European terrestrials with tubers, such as *Dactylorhiza, Orchis, Ophrys* or *Himatoglossum*

1. **Remove plant from pot.**

2. **Remove dead roots and wash.**

3. **Fill the pot to half-full with fine-grade pumice or 'Seramis®'. Place the tuber in the centre of the pot.**

4. **Fill around the roots with a compost of fine-grade pumice or quartz gravel and perlite.**

5. **Cover the crown of shoots with a mound of fine-grade pumice.**

6. **Infill the rest of the pot with composted wood or bark and quartz gravel and perlite. Water well.**

Cultivation in the garden

Pleione limprichtii

Hardy orchids can be versatile additions to gardens of many different types and sizes, from container gardens to green roofs. They fit well into many different planting schemes including wildlife gardens, formal flower beds, rock gardens, or gardens with a Chinese or Mediterranean theme.

Location and soil

Despite their obvious suitability for both the plants themselves and their mycorrhizal fungi, we do not recommend introducing orchids into sites where orchids are already growing naturally. To do so, would be to introduce the danger of disease. Also, if the introduced orchids are of the same species as the natural population, interbreeding is likely to bring alien genes into the natural population.

Some hardy orchids grow perfectly well when transferred to garden soil, provided it is not artificially fertilised. But almost all orchids will benefit from the addition of horticultural grit or other material to improve drainage and perlite to retain a suitable degree of moisture around the roots. Most orchids are intolerant of composts that include organic material in any quantity, but can otherwise be grown in a wide variety of composts. The pH range tolerated varies between orchid species. Orchids that tolerate a wide range of pH, such as *Dactylorhiza* and *Epipactis* species, adapt most easily to a garden setting.

Imported soil could be used to construct raised or sunken beds that imitate dry calcareous, moist calcareous, moist acidic or bog habitats, thereby providing a range of diverse habitats that can accommodate a wide variety of species.

Planting out

Orchids can establish well whether planted during periods of active growth or while dormant. Water the orchids in their pots thoroughly before planting out, remove the surface layer of

▲ *Epipactis* **Sabine**

▲ **Dactylorhizas adapt well to a garden setting**

vegetation in the planting spot, and use a bulb planter to make a hole the same size as the pot, then fill the hole with water. When planting, include all the compost from the pot to minimise root disturbance. Cover the planted area with leaf litter or a small wire cage to discourage excavation by small mammals. If the garden soil is poorly drained, planting in a depression or a dip should be avoided as the hole will fill with water causing the orchid to rot. In this case, you might consider planting the orchids in a raised bed.

Newly planted seedlings need watering for several years until they are well established and may need protection from slugs and snails. Continued management is required to maintain the low-nutrient status of the soil. In grassland areas, this would include seasonal mowing or animal grazing after the orchids have set seed. Cuttings must be removed if the grassland is mown. Grazing makes holes in the grass, enabling colonisation by orchid seedlings. In wooded habitats, it may be necessary to remove leaf litter. Scrub clearance and weeding will prevent plants from being overgrown, and coppicing and removal of trees will allow light in.

37

Choosing orchids for your garden

When choosing which orchids to grow, consider the natural habitats of your preferred species and select sites that match their wild habitats as closely as possible. Choose species to fit existing locations or make modifications to accommodate the species you desire. Hybrids are often more vigorous and easier to grow than their parental species and are becoming more widely available.

Orchids that can grow outside in a temperate climate such as that of the UK need to withstand winter frost and summer rain. Northern European species are obvious candidates for temperate gardens and local floras will indicate appropriate native species. Some Mediterranean, South African and South American species can also be grown if winter protection is provided.

The growth habits of the plants should also be considered. For example, if you wish to plant small areas relatively densely for visual impact, then consider planting tuberous species such as *Anacamptis laxiflora, A. morio, Dactylorhiza fuchsii, D. praetermissa, Ophrys apifera* and *Serapias lingua*. These have been successfully planted at 20 plants per square metre (2 plants per sq ft) at Wakehurst Place. By contrast, rhizomatous plants will benefit from more space to spread underground. *Ophrys apifera* and *Spiranthes spiralis* have flat rosettes that survive well in closely mown grass or bare soil areas.

Orchids are famed for their delicate flowers but some, such as *Gymnadenia* and *Spiranthes* species, are also scented. White-flowered species are visible by moonlight, adding a further attractive quality.

A very successful bog garden that showcases native orchids in a naturalistic setting, which includes carnivorous plants, has been created at Atlanta Botanical Garden in the USA

▼

Dactylorhiza maculata **thrives in marshy places**

▼

Woodland and shady places

Many hardy orchids prefer to grow in shaded places under small trees, shrubs or hedges. Species and hybrids of *Dactylorhiza*, *Orchis*, *Cypripedium*, *Epipactis* (*E. helleborine*), *Calanthe* and *Bletilla* all thrive in dappled light. Many shade-loving orchids appear to thrive when planted close to tree roots, possibly because of shared mycorrhizae.

Calanthe hybrids are seldom seen planted out in the UK. They can form large clumps in sheltered places, but may need further protection from winter wet. *Cymbidium goeringii* is also hardy and can be grown successfully in a sheltered spot.

Epipactis helleborine, a shade-loving species

Bogs and marginal areas

A number of orchid species love to have their feet wet, especially those that grow in marshes and on the margins of streams, ponds and lakes. Some species of *Dactylorhiza*, *Epipactis* (*E. gigantea*, *E. palustris* and *E. royleana*), *Spiranthes* (*S. cernua* and *S. sinensis*) and *Anacamptis* (*A. laxiflora* and *A. palustris*), together with *Cypripedium reginae*, thrive in marshy places. *Epipactis gigantea* 'Serpentine Night' and *Spiranthes cernua* var. *odorata* 'Chadd's Ford' can form magnificent clumps in a marshy spot.

Rock, scree and gravel gardens

Some orchids, especially those species with tubers, thrive in scree and gravel beds and on rock gardens. Species of *Anacamptis*, *Himantoglossum*, *Ophrys* and *Orchis* prefer the free-draining neutral or alkaline conditions that can be provided in such sites. *Dactylorhiza* hybrids look particularly fine growing on a rock garden. Geneva Botanic Garden had magnificent clumps of *Cypripedium reginae* and *C. calceolus* growing on its rock garden with their rhizomes tucked down in a damp hollow amongst the rock. *Cypripedium* hybrids can also thrive in such places.

Peat beds

Pleione limprichtii and some of its hybrids can be planted on a vertical side of a peat bed with the pseudobulbs well covered. Some marsh orchids, such as *Dactylorhiza maculata* and *Dactylorhiza* hybrids will also thrive here. *Cypripedium reginae* will also thrive in a damp peat bed.

Ophrys tenthredinifera growing on limestone ▶

Herbaceous borders

Dactylorhiza elata, *D. praetermissa*, *Dactylorhiza* hybrids and *Bletilla striata* are probably the orchids found most frequently in more formal borders. In the UK, the fine *Dactylorhiza foliosa* needs more frost protection, but produces a magnificent spectacle in a frost-free place. Increasingly, *Cypripedium* hybrids are being planted in borders, particularly in shadier places. They form large showy clumps when grown in suitable sites.

Living roofs

A number of European and North American species have been successfully grown in living roofs, an idea that has been taken up increasingly as a sustainable way of insulating a roof. In Europe, dactylorhizas and cypripediums have been used in roof-planting schemes with some success.

Growing conditions for wild hardy orchids

	Winter-green species	Summer-green tuberous species	Summer-green rhizomatous species
Climate preference	Adapted to warmer climates in the south of the UK, most species from this group are from southern Europe	Adapted to a climate with colder winters and higher spring rainfall, some species occur as far north as Scotland	Adapted to cooler climates
Planting density	20 plants per m² (2 plants per sq ft)	20 plants per m² (2 plants per sq ft)	10 plants per m² (1 plant per sq ft)
Mowing period	June to September	September to February	September to February
Water requirements	Do not allow to dry out rapidly	Intolerant of drying out during the dormant period, must be kept moist	No resistance to drying out, prefers wet habitats
Examples	*Anacamptis, Ophrys, Orchis, Serapias* and *Himantoglossum*	*Dactylorhiza, Gymnadenia* and *Platanthera*	*Cypripedium, Epipactis, Cephalanthera* and *Goodyera*

▶ **Dactylorhiza fuchsii**

Photo Ferran Pestaña

Anacamptis pyramidalis

Naturalising orchids

Restoring species-rich grassland

Some success in producing herb-rich meadows has been achieved in western Europe in recent years, even on land that has been intensively cultivated or managed for hay. When preparing the site, the nutrient levels in the substrate must be reduced, usually by removing the sod and topsoil.

If the basal rock is near the surface, as it is in some limestone areas, then orchids can establish very quickly. If the soils are deeper, then a strategy of spreading freshly cut hay from a nearby species-rich meadow can provide a seed source for a diverse meadow flora. A meadow that already contains orchids is an ideal seed source. Species such as *Dactylorhiza fuchsii*, *D. praetermissa*, *Platanthera bifolia*, *P. chlorantha* and *Anacamptis pyramidalis* are common enough in some areas of Europe to appear relatively frequently after such a treatment. Adding freshly collected seed of suitable species should enhance a site where the seed source lacks orchids, but remember that appropriate permissions must be sought before collecting seed in the wild for such purposes. The meadows must then be managed by cutting for hay after the orchids have set seed, usually in late July or early August.

The addition of seed of yellow rattle (*Rhinanthus* species) to grassland or meadow-land will improve the survival of orchids. Rattles are hemi-parasites on the roots of grasses and reduce their ability to compete with orchids and other plants that are intolerant of competition.

Common spotted orchids (Dactylorhiza fuchsii) and yellow rattle in a meadow

Dactylorhiza praetermissa on Chobham common, Surrey, UK

Enhancing a natural or semi-natural site

On a smaller scale, orchid seed, seedlings or flowering plants can be successfully introduced into existing grassland, meadows or unimproved lawns. The sod should be removed in limited areas or strips to remove competition and lower nutrient levels. Seeds can be scattered on the bare soils and left to germinate and grow. If conditions are suitable, flowering can occur as soon as three or four years after sowing.

Where *Dactylorhiza fuchsii* and *D. praetermissa* grow in gardens, they often seed into pots or bare areas in the garden. These plants should be potted with as little disturbance to the soil as possible. They need regular watering, preferably with rainwater, for one or two years after planting until they become become fully established.

Orchids in lawns should not be mown until they have set and shed seed in late July or August. This, unfortunately, leaves the lawn with an untidy appearance with the orchids in high grass surrounded by lawn that has been cut as usual. However, the rapid increase of species such as *Ophrys apifera*, *Dactylorhiza fuchsii* and *Epipactis helleborine* under such a regime is immensely satisfying.

Christopher Lloyd has naturalised *Orchis mascula* in his orchard at Great Dixter with great success. Once established, the orchids benefitted from a regime that let the fruits mature and release seed before the orchard was mown.

The success of such methods is exemplified by a large arable area near Courgenay in the Jura in Switzerland. This area was selected for restoration to herb-rich grassland as part compensation for the building of a nearby motorway. The area had previously been used to grow maize for a number of years. The regime adopted was to scrape the top-soil from the site down to its limestone base-rock, sow commercially available wild-flower seed and let the seed from surrounding areas naturally vegetate the area. Within five years, large colonies of *Ophrys fuciflora* had established on the site, and other orchids, such as *Anacamptis pyramidalis* had also appeared.

▲ *Dactylorhiza x grandis* **in the rock garden at Kew**

Several County Naturalists' Trusts use grazing, usually by cattle in the autumn and winter months, to break up the sod in orchid-rich meadows in order to provide suitable places for orchid seed to germinate, thereby increasing the orchid population.

Orchids that grow naturally in gardens

A number of species occur naturally in gardens in the UK and Europe. In the UK, *Dactylorhiza fuchsii*, *Epipactis helleborine*, *Ophrys apifera* and *Orchis mascula* are perhaps those that most frequently appear in gardens, usually in disturbed soil or in rough grass and hedgerows. All can be successfully increased by a suitable management regime, usually by leaving grass cutting until after the seed capsules of the orchids have dehisced. Pollinating some flowers artificially can also increase seed numbers significantly.

Suitable companion plants

Orchids can be successfully grown with many other garden plants. Less vigorous foliage plants, especially some ferns, can set off the orchid flowers to perfection. The less vigorous bulbous plants are also good companions, especially *Arisaema*, *Arum*, *Erythronium*, *Podophyllum*, *Trillium* and smaller hostas.

 ***Cypripedium* hybrids in a garden**

43

Pests and diseases

Ants farming aphids

The three keys to effective control of pests and diseases are good hygiene, regular inspection of your plants, and prompt action as soon as any hint of a problem is found.

Physical removal

Slugs and snails are probably the most serious pest and they can usually be found after a thorough search. Many insect pests can often be easily removed using a soft paint brush, perhaps dipped in a weak detergent solution or methylated spirits (rubbing alcohol).

Pests often cause problems at certain times of the year or in particular weather conditions. Insect pests reproduce more rapidly when temperatures are warm and may be killed by very low winter temperatures. Slugs and snails are much more active and problematic when the weather is wet.

Biological control or chemical control?

If purely physical removal techniques fail to cure your pest problem, you may wish to resort to chemical or biological control. Both methods have their own advantages and disadvantages. Frequent use of insecticides can lead to the rapid evolution of resistant pests and so it is a good idea to rotate different insecticides if you decide to use them. You should avoid spraying with any type of insecticide in bright sunlight, as the residual moisture on the leaves can lead to scorching of the foliage. Biological control methods often require continuing low levels of infestation to sustain the controlling parasite.

Safety note

When using insecticides, always read the manufacturer's instructions carefully before use and follow them carefully.

▲ An adult ladybird can eat about 5,000 aphids. Adult ladybirds, larvae, attractants and even ladybird houses can all be bought to help with biocontrol.

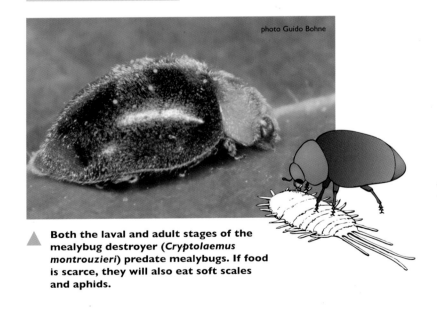

photo Guido Bohne

▲ Both the laval and adult stages of the mealybug destroyer (*Cryptolaemus montrouzieri*) predate mealybugs. If food is scarce, they will also eat soft scales and aphids.

Aphids

Newly potted orchid seedlings are particularly vulnerable to aphid attack, especially when growing in a glasshouse or polytunnel where these insects are encouraged by warmer conditions.

More familiarly known as greenfly or blackfly, aphids are sap-sucking insects that can damage plants either directly or by transmitting viruses. They are most frequently found clustered on tender young shoots or flower buds. They also secrete a sweet sticky solution called honeydew, which encourages the growth of unsightly and damaging sooty moulds.

There are a range of possible solutions to aphid attack. Newly potted seedlings should be kept separate from mature plants to avoid infestation. Alternatively, they can be covered in a 'tent' of agricultural fleece as a barrier. Minor infestations can be squashed or rubbed from the shoots and buds with the fingers and thumb.

Most insecticides will control aphids. Gardeners can choose between spraying with synthetic insecticides, such as contact-action bifenthrin, or a systemic chemical, such as imidacloprid. Alternatively, you may choose to use sprays that are derived from natural substances such as pyrethrum or fatty acids and vegetable oils.

Aphids have many natural enemies, including adult ladybirds and their larvae, hoverfly larvae, lacewing larvae and several parasitic wasps. The parasitic wasp *Aphidius* will reduce but not eradicate the problem. *Aphidoletes* (gall-midge) can also be used against aphids.

Ants

Although they seldom damage plants directly, ants should be discouraged in the greenhouse because they will carry aphids, which they then 'farm' for their honeydew, onto your plants. There are a range of proprietary products on the

Grower's tip

Be aware that manufacturers may not test their products specifically for possible toxic effects on orchids. Pesticides should always be used with caution as they may cause damage. Seedlings are particularly vulnerable and should always be removed from the glasshouse before spraying. Some orchid genera are more sensitive than others. *Himantoglossum*, for example, is particularly sensitive to insecticides, even when plants are mature.

market for controlling ants, including powders, baits, sprays and aerosols. Most are not suitable for greenhouse use, although ant baits ('traps') can be effective.

Birds and small mammals

Birds and small mammals (mice) can be a problem in the garden. They can also enter the greenhouse, where mice in particular may find the winter conditions to their liking. In the garden, chicken wire or netting can be placed over plants to deter birds and small mammals that may nibble the plants or inadvertently dig them up.

Bees

More of a nuisance than a pest, bees (particularly bumblebees) and other insects can cause a problem by pollinating orchid flowers and thereby reducing their longevity. They can be kept out of the greenhouse by placing mesh over greenhouse vents.

False spider mites

So-called because they do not spin a web (see red spider mites), false spider mites (*Brevipalpus oncidii*) can cause considerable damage to *Pleione* plants in particular. Scarcely visible to the naked eye, the grower may be unaware of the presence of these mites unless they dig up the pseudobulbs and examine them closely underneath a hand lens. False spider mites produce toxic saliva, the first symptoms of a problem often being that plants fail to thrive. The pseudobulbs will then become progressively smaller with each passing year and will produce fewer and fewer flowers. Although false spider mites can affect

Grower's tip

An interval of a few weeks should be left between spraying and introducing biological control as insecticidal chemicals can harm the biological control agents. Do not use fatty acids at the same time as biological control as they are also damaging to the controlling parasites.

all plant parts, they prefer the undersides of the pseudobulbs of *Pleione*, where they lay their eggs in cracks and crevices.

By re-potting your *Pleione* in fresh compost each year (which in any case is good horticultural practice) you have an opportunity to inspect the pseudobulbs for mites and their eggs. The pseudobulbs can be cleaned and, if necessary, treated with an insecticide.

Mealy bugs

Mealybugs are easily identified by their white waxy coats and their resemblance to miniature armadillos. Although they may be discovered on any part of a plant, they are fond of hiding in the crevices of leaf axils or in the crowns, where the damage they cause can lead to wet rots setting in. Mealybugs can be eliminated using insecticides, but are easily removed with a soft paintbrush dipped in methylated spirit (rubbing alcohol).

Red spider mites

Almost invisible to the naked eye, these tiny members of the spider family are more easily seen with the aid of a magnifying glass. They thrive in warm, dry conditions. Although often thought of as a greenhouse pest, they can also infest plants in the garden during hot, dry summers. The symptoms of spider mite infestation begin with a typical silvery sheen to the undersides of leaves. In serious infestations, this develops into a fine silk webbing. Warmer-growing orchids, such as *Calanthe* species and their hybrids, are particularly susceptible, as are *Cymbidium* species.

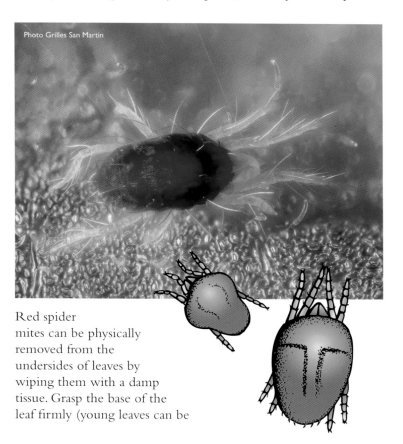

Photo Grilles San Martin

Red spider mites can be physically removed from the undersides of leaves by wiping them with a damp tissue. Grasp the base of the leaf firmly (young leaves can be pulled out of the plant all too easily) and wipe the leaf from the base towards the tip. Alternatively, pesticides approved for use by home gardeners against red spider mite include fatty acids (insecticidal soaps) and vegetable oils that work by blocking the mites' breathing tubes, preventing respiration. Biological control with the predatory mite *Phytoseiulus persimilis* is now widely used in commercial glasshouses where tomatoes and cucumbers are raised, as red spider mites have become resistant to many chemical controls.

Scale insects

Adult scale insects are easily recognised as they resemble miniature limpets. The eggs hatch beneath their protective umbrellas into tiny transparent 'crawlers'. Almost impossible to spot with the naked eye, they spread from one plant to another. The crawlers are probably the stage at which scale insects are most vulnerable to insecticides. The adults, with their protective coat, can only be dealt with by using a systemic insecticide.

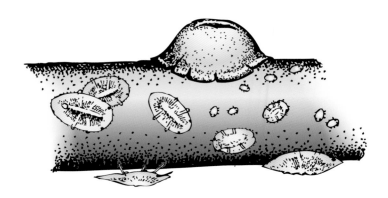

Prompt action and physical removal are the keys to success. With patience and persistence, they are relatively easy to eliminate after a number of treatments.

Slugs and snails

There is nothing more galling than walking up the garden early in the morning only to discover that the plants that you have lovingly nurtured for so long have been decimated by the local molluscs overnight. Slugs and snails top any list of garden pests, having the ability to cause considerable damage even to mature plants in just one evening, and to consume a tray of seedlings at a single sitting. They are creatures of habit and it is often possible to find a culprit by following its tell-tail silvery trail back to its daytime hiding place. As they are mainly active at night, they can often be found by going around the garden or into the greenhouse in the late evening and searching for them with a torch (flashlight).

Slugs like to curl up in the bottoms of pots, but a piece of zinc or other mesh covering the drainage holes in the base will prevent them entering the compost and feeding on the roots. Coarse grit placed around orchid plants can act as a deterrent. In the garden, copper rings can deter slugs and snails to some extent. Some people swear by beer and cider traps. If you favour biological control methods, then you might consider trying watering with a suspension of nematode worms (*Phasmarhabditis hermaphrodita*). These worms invade the bodies of their molluscan hosts and release deadly bacteria. They require that the soil or compost is moist and the temperature at least 5 °C (41 °F). The use of blue, toxic metaldehyde pellets is not recommended if young children and pets might encounter them.

Tortrix moth caterpillars

Less familiar pests of hardy orchids include *Tortrix* moth caterpillars. These can be simply picked off the foliage or sprayed with *Bacillus thuringiensis* (Bt), a common soil bacterium with unusual properties that make it useful for pest control in certain situations. It is the only 'microbial insecticide' in widespread use, and acts by producing toxic proteins that react with the lining of the gut of susceptible insects.

Woodlice

Commonly called 'pill bugs' or 'slaters', these little crustaceans are usually more of a nuisance than a menace. Hiding in cool, damp and dark places beneath plant pots or in debris under greenhouse staging, they normally feed on decaying vegetable matter. Nevertheless they should be discouraged as they have a fondness for nibbling the soft tissue of seedlings and the tips of new roots. Rather than using chemical pesticides the best way to get rid of them is by practising good greenhouse hygiene.

Viruses

Cypripedium are susceptible to 'Potti virus', which is indicated by yellow streaks on the leaves. Viruses can be carried by orchid seeds but can be eliminated through meristem culture. Nutrient deficiency can produce similar symptoms and the nutrient status of plants should be tested before they are discarded and destroyed. *Dactylorhiza* orchids are also sometimes susceptible to viruses.

Raising orchids from seed to flowering plant

Cypripedium macranthos

An understanding of each species' life cycle is vital to those wishing to cultivate hardy and near-hardy orchids. How an orchid survives through its dormant season is of considerable importance to growers. In climates where the winter is both damp and cold, such as that of northern Europe including the UK, more orchids are lost when dormant during the winter months than at any other time. This is often due to prevailing damp, rather than cold, conditions. Many orchids will survive periods when temperatures are low if kept dry (but not desiccated) but will rapidly perish if the tubers are too moist.

The yearly cycle of most hardy orchids can be divided into an active growing season and a season of more or less marked dormancy. Active growth usually occurs when the weather is moist and mild.

In the Mediterranean, temperate Australia and regions with similar climates, the active phase runs from late autumn, when the rains begin, through winter until early spring. Leaf growth and the build-up of food reserves in the roots and tubers are usually completed by the time the flowering spike develops in the spring. Consequently, plants that are moved during the flowering period often transplant successfully. Seed set completes the cycle by late spring or early summer and the orchids enter a dry-season dormant period. Most *Ophrys* and *Barlia* species follow this cycle.

Further north and at higher elevations, the severe winter weather and frequent frosts preclude growth during winter. There, vegetative growth starts in the milder spring weather as soil temperatures rise, with flowering occurring in late spring and summer. Seed is shed in the late summer or autumn as the orchid enters its cold-induced dormancy. *Cypripedium, Dactylorhiza, Gymnadenia, Platanthera* and *Epipactis* species follow this pattern in Europe and temperate North America.

Grower's tip

If you are a beginner, it is a good idea to buy some plants that are large enough to flower at the outset of your new hobby.

Protocorms ▶

Young seedlings ▶

Cypripedium **seedlings for winter storage** ▶

Newly potted *Cypripedium* **hybrid seedlings** ▶

51

Growing orchids from seed

It is possible to produce your own hardy orchid plants from seed at home without the need for specialist laboratory equipment. We strongly recommend however, that anyone who is attempting to propagate orchids at home for the first time should talk to others who have already had some success. This is most easily achieved by joining a local enthusiasts' group or a national society, such as the UK Hardy Orchid Society (HOS).

Hardy Orchid Society members can also purchase materials from the society's seed and fungus bank, obtain supplies of certain media and access a wealth of information, mainly written by successful amateur growers. The early editions of the HOS newsletter are a particularly valuable source of information for propagators, with many articles describing how to construct your own glove boxes or laminar flow cabinets, easy methods of growing from seed and even a simplified way to isolate potentially symbiotic fungus from your own cultivated orchids' roots. Detailed accounts of general home-growing or laboratory techniques can be obtained from publications such as *Growing Orchids from Seed* by Philip Seaton and Margaret Ramsay (2005).

Why grow your own orchids from seed?

There are a number of compelling reasons for growing orchids from seed:

- Some species are otherwise difficult or impossible to obtain.

- Adult plants often do not transplant easily and cultivated material is easier to grow.

- It can can be achieved using nothing more complicated than the equipment found in any domestic kitchen and the simplest of culture media.

- Few things in orchid growing give more satisfaction than raising your own plants from seed, and many of the more common species are relatively easy.

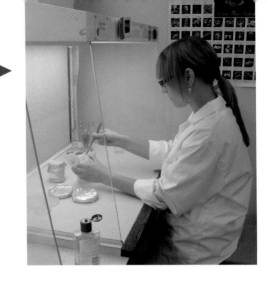

Sowing seed in a laminar flow hood ▶

Sowing from seed can provide large numbers of plants and allow you to breed your own hybrids

▼

Obtaining seed

Orchid seed can be obtained from a number of sources:

- Collect it yourself from the wild. Local and national laws must be followed when contemplating orchid seed collection. Permission of the land-owner is also a pre-requisite where seed collecting is legally permitted.

- Purchase from a reputable seed supplier.

- Membership of a specialist society. For example, in the UK, orchid seeds can be obtained from the Alpine Garden Society seed exchange scheme and the HOS maintains a seed bank for its members.

- Hand pollination of your own plants.

▲ **Ideally, orchid seed should be stored in glass, screwtop vials**

▲ **Mature *Cypripedium* capsule splits to release thousands of seeds**

Seed quality and storage

Only use good-quality seed that has a high percentage of seeds containing viable embryos. The quality of the seed will depend on a number of factors including the pollination event, the environmental conditions as the seed capsules mature, and how the seed has been harvested and stored after harvest. If you wish to store some of your own harvested seed for the future, seed viability can be maintained by keeping the seed clean and dry in a sealed (preferably glass) container. (Saving some seed is always a good idea in case, for example, your flasks become contaminated or you wish to sow some seed again.) Good quality seed will often retain its viability for many years if stored under these conditions in a domestic refrigerator at a temperature of around 5 °C (41 °F).

Seed sterilisation

Orchid seeds must be sterilised to remove from their surface any bacterial or fungal spores that would rapidly grow on contact with the medium and overwhelm the seed. Seed sterilisation also helps to break seed dormancy by softening the seed coat. This is especially important for hardy orchid seeds, which frequently require a longer sterilisation period than epiphytic orchid seeds and sometimes additional treatments (e.g. acid or chilling) to break dormancy.

Sodium hypochlorite is usually the sterilant of choice, and this is readily available in commercial bleach solutions such as Domestos®. Concentrations of between 0.1 and 1.5% available chlorine for 15–30 minutes are most commonly used. Placing the seeds in a filter paper packet makes them easier to handle during sterilisation.

Once sterilised, the seeds must be sown under sterile conditions. When available, laminar flow benches which the filter air to remove microorganisms, provide an ideal environment for seed sowing. Alternatively, glove boxes or simple covers such as upended fish tanks are adequate, and even working on an open bench is possible provided that there are no draughts and attention is paid to working in a sterile manner.

Some growers prefer to use seeds from immature green capsules because these seeds often germinate quicker than mature seeds. Contamination by environmental fungi and bacteria can also be less when immature seeds that have remained within a capsule are used. In this case, the whole capsule is first surface-sterilised in bleach, then dipped in alcohol and passed briefly through a flame. The capsule is then cut open and the seeds spread on the surface of the medium under sterile conditions.

Green *Dactylorhiza* capsules

Ensuring germination

Some hardy orchids can be grown successfully in flasks on a simple low-nutrient medium with an appropriate symbiotic fungus. Plant development is usually faster when a suitable fungus is present than in an asymbiotic system, and symbiotic growth provides better survival rates when moving the plants from the flask to the pot. A simple oat medium suitable for germination can be made from 3.5 g powdered porridge oats, 6 g agar and 0.1 g yeast extract (some have used 'Marmite') dissolved in 1 litre of hot water and sterilised in a pressure cooker.

Seedling care

Most terrestrial orchid seeds require dark conditions for germination and early development because their seedlings are light sensitive. A dark cupboard can be used to exclude light. Alternatively, a tray of Petri dishes or flasks can be placed in black plastic refuse bag or wrapped in foil.

Once the seedlings have developed strong shoots, most can utilise light for photosynthesis. At this stage, a 16-hour light/8-hour dark light pattern is often used, but some species could probably benefit from a light regime that follows natural conditions more closely; for instance, species that naturally prefer deep shade are likely to grow best in relatively low light and cooler temperatures. The growth of hardy orchid seedlings may well be influenced strongly by both day length (or artificial photoperiod when growing under lights) and temperature.

Optimum temperatures for growth *in vitro* are generally around 20 °C (68 °F). But many temperate orchids, especially those grown with mycorrhizal fungi, do not grow well at temperatures above 20 °C (68 °F), and regimes of 12–15 °C (54–59 °F) or even lower can stimulate the healthy seedling growth of some species (e.g. *Ophrys* species). Some seeds require a cold period (0–4 °C/32–39 °F), or alternating cycles of cold and warmer temperatures, in order to break dormancy.

Symbiotic and asymbiotic propagation

Under natural conditions, many orchids rely on partnerships with saprophytic fungi to meet their nutritional needs. These can be replicated *in vitro* by growing orchids on a simple oats medium with appropriate fungi. Alternatively, the nutrients that would be supplied by the fungi can be added to the medium. These means of growing orchids are referred to as symbiotic (with fungi) and asymbiotic (without fungi) propagation.

An asymbiotic orchid medium is basically a sugar and fertiliser solution, with a gelling agent (agar) added to give a firm surface for sowing. Developing orchid seedlings require the same basic nutrients as any growing plant: nitrogen (N), phosphorus (P), potassium (K) and magnesium (Mg). Other minerals, such as manganese, calcium and boron, might be required in trace amounts.

A wide range of media have been developed for the cultivation of orchid seedlings, but most species and genera will germinate on a comparatively narrow range of media. Several are now available pre-packaged from a number of different suppliers. These include Murashige and Skoog (which should be used at ½ or ¼ strength), TGZ-SL, Phytamax, and Malmgren's medium (which contains complex organic molecules in the form of amino acids and vitamins). Many growers have found that the addition of small amounts of organic substances, such as pineapple juice, potato, swede, coconut water or banana, is beneficial.

Orchids can be propagated on agar medium in a variety of sterile containers

Many species of orchid, particularly those from cooler northern hemisphere habitats require cooling (during which vernalisation occurs) to initiate different stages of growth. For these species, tuber development, breaking of bud dormancy and the formation of leaves are stimulated by a cold treatment of 8–12 weeks at 4–5 °C (39–41 °F) or less (although freezing of the tissues should be avoided). Vernalisation may also synchronise the emergence of the leaves and inflorescences of summer-green European species. Stimulating seedling development is particularly important before seedlings can be moved from the growth room to the greenhouse or cold frame.

Each genus and species is likely to differ slightly in its requirements for optimum germination and subsequent seedling development. Many growers have their own individual and favourite modifications. There is no single correct way of raising your orchids from seed, indeed one of the joys of raising orchids is their variability. Nevertheless, we believe that the advice contained in the following sections will lead to success and provide a sound basis for the cultivation of more challenging species.

Seedlings growing in a fridge ▶

▲ **Some growers incorporate potato cubes into the medium for *Cypripedium* seedlings**

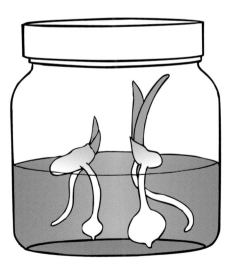

▲ ***Ophrys* seedlings produce characteristic 'sinkers' that swell into tubers**

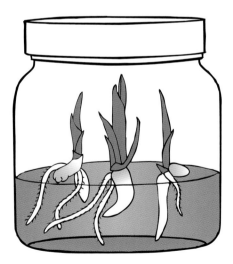

▲ **Jars with clear tops increase the light available to these *Dactylorhiza* seedlings**

Dactylorhiza

Dactylorhiza elata

Dactylorhiza is essentially a northern genus and thus requires little, if any, winter protection. In nature, many species grow in habitats where they are watered with mineral-rich and often limey water. As a result, the plants respond well to being watered with tap water (rather than rainwater). The seed is relatively easy to germinate and can grow into flowering plants within three years.

Life cycle of the common spotted orchid (*Dactylorhiza fuchsii*)

Like other typical members of the genus, *Dactylorhiza fuchsii* is 'summer-green'. The shoots emerge in the spring and the leaves remain green over the warmer, moist summer months before dying down as autumn approaches, the days become shorter and temperatures fall. The underground tubers and roots are replaced annually.

Dactylorhiza fuchsii ▶

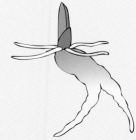

March

The shoot typically emerges above ground in late March or early April. The greyish-green elliptical-oblong leaves gradually increase in size and number, forming a basal rosette that remains green throughout the winter and spring. White adventitious roots become visible as bumps beneath the leaf sheath above the tuber.

April and May

The roots lengthen and the tuber begins to shrink as its food reserves are mobilised towards the expanding leaves. A new tuber begins to form and can be seen as a small white protuberance on the stem above the old tuber.

June and July

Plants that are large enough to flower bloom in June or July. The old tuber continues to shrivel as its reserves are utilised in producing additional leaves

and, if the tuber is large enough, a flower spike. The new tuber enlarges and eventually bursts through the leaf sheath. The roots are generally brown and begin to die by the time of flowering in June. They are dead and shrivelled by the end of the summer.

August

By autumn, the leaves have died down and the new tuber enters into the dormant state in which it will remain throughout the winter. New root growth can happen as long as the temperatures do not dip too low.

Seed harvest

Ideally, mature seed should be collected at the point when the seed capsule splits or immediately before. *Dactylorhiza* capsules take just 6−9 weeks to mature, turning brown before splitting and releasing 10,000 or more seeds from each capsule. Seed should be dried as soon as possible after collection (oven-dried rice is recommended as a suitable desiccant), and then placed in a sealed tube for storage in a cool place: ideally in a refrigerator at around 4°C (39 °F) or a freezer at around −18 °C (0 °F).

Sowing immature seed

Some growers prefer to sow immature seed from a green capsule, using the so-called 'green pod' method. This produces quicker results and avoids the problems of contamination by environmental bacteria or fungi that can occur with surface-sterilised mature seed, but immature seed cannot usually be stored for sowing later. If growers wish to avoid the need to disinfect mature seed, then an intact seed capsule from 2−5 cm (1−2") or so above the first naturally dehiscing pod will probably be a good source of seed for immediate sowing.

Mature *Dactylorhiza* seed do not, however, have any significant dormancy factors that prevent their germination soon after collection, and thus the 'green pod' technique is not as useful for this genus as it is for others.

Sowing mature seed

Symbiotic germination

Dactylorhiza seedlings can be easily grown on an oat medium using a suitable symbiotic fungus. By comparison with asymbiotic techniques, symbiotic germination produces more vigorous plants that develop more quickly and probably transplant to soil more successfully. But large-scale propagation is achieved more easily using asymbiotic methods. Perhaps the biggest problem for those wishing

▲

Seed capsules of
Dactylorhiza

to use a symbiotic technique is obtaining a suitable fungus for each genus or species. Membership of organisations such as the Hardy Orchid Society may resolve this problem to some extent by enabling growers to meet others with similar interests (and different fungi).

Fungi can lose their effectiveness with repeated sub-culture on an oats medium alone (i.e. if they are not used to infect an orchid protocorm), although sub-culture on fungal isolating medium can reduce the likelihood of this possibility. Whenever possible, we recommend obtaining a culture of a fungus that is already stimulating germination of the relevant species.

Method

1. Sow seed in the autumn on oat medium with fungus. Culture B1, a fungus isolated by Jim Hill, appears to be one of the best available for *Dactylorhiza*. It does not tend to lose its vigour and works consistently for most species.

2. Keep the cultures at room temperature until the seed has germinated (usually within 3–5 weeks).

3. Prick the protocorms out onto fresh oat medium in Petri dishes or honey jars at a rate of 4–8 protocorms per vessel.

4. Maintain the cultures at room temperature (or slightly cooler) for about another month to allow the transplanted protocorms to fatten up.

5. Refrigerate for 3 months over the winter.

6. Plant the protocorms into compost immediately after taking the cultures out of the fridge. Although they consist of little more than large vernalised protocorms with large shoot buds, the symbiotic seedlings can be successfully weaned into suitable compost. The compost can be heat sterilised immediately before weaning, but successful growth will usually occur in un-sterilised composts. Plunge the pots in a cold frame outside for a period of about 6 months.

7. Small leaves rapidly appear as the spring progresses but underground root growth is much more marked. Root growth culminates at the end of the summer in the production of small, elongated, finger-like or digitate tubers.

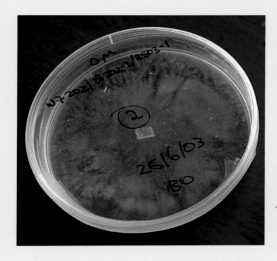

Fungus culture suitable for germination of *Dactylorhiza* growing in a petri dish

***Dactylorhiza* protocorms transplanted onto fresh agar. Transfer of no more than five widely spaced protocorms will allow each sufficient nutrients for maximal growth.**

Seed of *Dactylorhiza praetermissa* as imaged using a scanning electron microscope

Asymbiotic germination

Mature seed germinates relatively easily on a wide range of asymbiotic media, including ½- or ¼-strength Murashige and Skoog or Phytamax, full-strength Malmgren's or full-strength TGZ-SL. The addition of pineapple juice at 2% and adjustment of the pH of the medium to 5.6–5.9 benefit this genus. Some species, such as *Dactylorhiza romana* and *D. aristata*, can prove more difficult to germinate asymbiotically than the more common Western European species, but this may simply reflect a shortage of good out-crossed seed.

Asymbiotically grown
***Dactylorhiza* in a flask**

Method

1 *Dactylorhiza* seed will only germinate in the dark. Petri dishes (or flasks if you prefer) can either be wrapped in foil or placed in a black plastic bag to keep out the light.

2 Sow seed thinly in the autumn and then refrigerate for 3 months over the winter.

3 Dark conditions must be maintained until the seed has germinated and the protocorms have begun to produce shoots. Cultures can be kept permanently in the dark until weaned. Remove from the refrigerator in the early spring and move the Petri dishes or flasks to a cool room (16–20 °C/61–68 °F).

4 All of the viable seeds should have germinated within two or three months of being removed from the fridge, in fact germination may have already begun during refrigeration. Prick out the protocorms onto fresh medium in a flask as soon as they are large enough to handle with a pair of fine forceps, leaving any remaining seeds to germinate and be transferred at a later date. If the protocorms are not transplanted early in their development (or if the seed has been sown too densely in the first place), they can rapidly form a tangled mat as their rhizoids begin to interweave. This makes them difficult or nigh on impossible to separate and inevitably leads to damage to many of the rhizoids as the protocorms are teased apart.

5 Asymbiotic seedlings can be re-plated at a higher density than is advisable for the symbiotic technique. Initially, up to 32 protocorms per honey jar is acceptable, but this density should be reduced to 16 per jar at later re-platings as the plants grow larger. Generally, the growing protocorms will benefit from media that contain a higher concentration of minerals and sugars than those used for sowing the seed. For example, protocorms grown from seed sown on ¼-strength 'Phytamax' with 10g/litre (1.3 oz/US gallon) sucrose can be moved on to ½-strength medium with 15g/litre (2oz/US gallon) sucrose. The medium in the flasks used for growing-

Asymbiotically grown *Dactylorhiza* seedlings that are almost ready for weaning can be exposed to weak light and allowed to green-up

on may also be rather deeper than before to allow space for root expansion. The very substantial root growth that is seen with genera like *Cypripedium* does not usually occur with *in vitro Dactylorhiza* seedlings during the first year. Nevertheless, some cultures on certain media might begin to produce elongated shoots and short leaves. Taller flasks, such as honey jars or 'Kilner' jars, allow more headroom for these seedlings to grow.

6 Seedlings may be moved on roughly every 3 months, although some growers re-plate at lower density and move the seedlings on only occasionally if at all.

7 There appears to be little if any benefit in exposing *Dactylorhiza* seedlings to light during their first year *in vitro*, although the shoots will grow and become green if you do.

8 Refrigerate the seedlings again for another 3 months when the second winter arrives.

9 After the seedlings have experienced their second period of refrigeration, the time has come to wean them into a suitable compost or soil. At this stage, chlorophyll production can be enabled by exposing flasks containing those plants with substantial leaf growth to weak light for a few weeks before moving them onto compost. This is not necessary for plants that have roots and large shoots but no substantial leaf growth, which should be moved straight to compost or soil.

10 Wean the seedlings into pots of appropriate compost and plunge the pots into damp sand or peat in a cold frame outside. It is not usually necessary to heat-sterilise the compost. It is, however, a very good idea to seed the compost with a proven symbiotic fungus at this stage, and this should help the small plants to survive. This may be done by chopping up the oat medium from half a petri dish of a culture of suitable fungus and incorporating it into the top 2 cm of compost in the pot. Alternatively, the seedlings can be planted out into soil around the roots of fully grown plants. As spring temperatures increase, the seedlings will sprout and produce leaf growth. For the first year in soil, most growth occurs underground in the root system: by the time autumn arrives, small, elongate and finger-like or typically digitate tubers will have formed. Using this method, the period from seed to weaning is about 18 months.

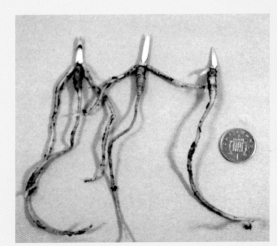

Dactylorhiza fuchsii 18 months after sowing seed

Potting on

In the late summer or autumn of their first year in compost or soil, the young dormant tubers of *Dactylorhiza* seedlings may be thinned out and moved into larger pots. These are best plunged in a damp peat or sand bed covered by a cold frame for the winter.

Composts

Most dactylorchid species and hybrids are damp-loving and like well-drained but water-retentive compost that has a relatively high organic content. Two composts that have been used with some success are:

- 3 parts fibrous loam, 2 parts composted bark fines, 2 parts coarse Perlite, 4 parts pine duff, and 4 or 5 parts coarse grit;

- 3 parts milled peat, 1 part loam, 1 part grit, and 2 parts sharp sand.

Composts with a low organic matter content have also been used successfully, but these require very frequent fertiliser use to ensure good growth. One such compost comprises:

6 parts coarse pumice, 5 parts coarse Perlite, 5 parts vermiculite, 1 part loam, and 1 part fine orchid bark. The loam can be omitted.

Pots

The choice of traditional clay or plastic pots is a matter of personal preference. One tried and tested method is to maintain the *Dactylorhiza* seedlings in plunged clay pots for the first few years and then pot them individually in plastic "long-tom" pots plunged in wet sharp sand when the plants reach flowering size.

Place plenty of drainage material in the bottom of the pot. As *Dactylorhiza* is a damp-loving genus, an absorbent material such as Seramis® or bark should be included in the drainage material to ensure that the compost above is never allowed to become dry. It is also a good idea to place a piece of net over the drainage holes to prevent entry of slugs.

Overwintering

Pots can be plunged in a bed of moist horticultural sand; mature plants can be left in the garden. *Dactylorhiza* is essentially a northern genus and little, if any, winter protection is necessary. Some species, such as *D. sambucina*, prefer a cold, dryish winter, but the majority of species and hybrids require no protection from winter rain, frost or snow and happily survive outside in most of northern Europe as long as they are plunged to prevent excessive short-term temperature variations.

Inspect the plants regularly for aphids, which can infest plants that are in leaf at any time of the year. If spotted early, aphids are easily removed with a moist soft paintbrush.

▼ **First-year seedlings of *Dactylorhiza maculata* are overwintered within a cold frame**

◀ **Dactylorhiza fuchsii
one-year-old seedlings**

During the summertime

Dactylorhiza plants can be maintained throughout the year in individual pots that are sunk in a damp sand plunge in a shade house. They can be transferred into the garden for the summer months, sinking the pots up to their rims in the garden soil. The leaves will gradually die down in the autumn as the plants enter their winter dormancy when they can then be returned to the shade house for winter protection.

Alternatively, plants can be transplanted into soil in a garden setting. Many dactylorchids are happy in the garden during the summer months although the diploid marsh orchids, in particular, really require a wetter environment than most gardens can provide.

Dactylorhiza will benefit from the use of organic fertilisers and some growers include John Innes No.2 or multi-purpose compost in their mixes because they contain extra nutrients. *Dactylorhiza* plants may be fertilised on occasions with ¼- or ½-strength organic fertilisers such as seaweed extract and fish emulsion. The composts in which *Dactylorhiza* are grown often contain a high proportion of organic material and have a tendency to lose their good drainage characteristics with time. Therefore, it is probably best to re-pot plants every second year at least.

Ophrys

Ophrys fuciflora

Ophrys seed is relatively easy to germinate asymbiotically. Depending on the species, flowering plants can be produced from seed within 3–5 years. Northern species are often relatively slow-growing.

Life cycle of the bee orchid (*Ophrys apifera*)

The life cycle of *Ophrys apifera* is typical for members of this genus, which are all 'winter-green'. The shoots emerge in the autumn and the leaves remain green over the cool, moist winter months. The above-ground parts of the plant die down and the tubers become dormant in the heat of the dry summertime. The underground tubers and roots are replaced annually.

Ophrys species are primarily adapted to a Mediterranean-type climate, with cool, moist winters and hot, dry summers. But winter-green *Ophrys* species are also found in more northerly regions where the winters are much colder, and the leaves of these species appear later in the year. The leaves grow slowly while temperatures are cool, but growth accelerates as temperatures increase in the spring. Most *Ophrys* species flower in the spring, whereas Northern species, such as *O. apifera*, flower a month or two later in June or July.

September

The shoot typically emerges above ground in September following rain and a sequence of cool nights. If there is sparse rainfall during the period from August to October, the emergence of shoots can be delayed until November or even early December. The greyish-green elliptical-oblong leaves gradually increase in size and number to form a basal rosette that remains green throughout the winter and spring. White adventitious roots become visible as bumps beneath the leaf sheath above the tuber.

November to May

A new tuber begins to form as a small white protuberance on the stem above the old tuber, eventually bursting through the leaf sheath. Growth is slow during the winter, but the tuber begins to grow rapidly in mid-March. Large plants can have 6–11 roots by April. By May, the new egg-shaped tuber is as large as, or larger than, the old tuber and the new roots have burst through the leaf sheath and are up to 2 cm (7/8") long.

June and July

Plants that have reached flowering size bloom in June or July just as the leaves begin to senesce. The old tuber begins to shrivel as its reserves are used up during flowering and the formation of the new tuber. The roots are generally brown and beginning to die by the time of flowering in June, and they are completely dead and shrivelled by late July. The seed capsules mature and turn brown before dehiscence, when each capsule may release many thousands of seeds. *Ophrys apifera* is unusual in that it is a self-pollinating orchid.

65

Seed harvest

Ideally, mature seed should be collected immediately prior to or at the point when the seed capsule splits. The seed should be dried, placed in a sealed tube and kept in a cool place: ideally in a refrigerator at around 4 °C (39 °F) or a freezer at around −18 °C (0 °F).

Sowing immature seed

Ophrys 'green pod' seed that is sufficiently mature to germinate successfully can be obtained by selecting the first unripe pod above one that is on the point of splitting.

Sowing mature seed

Asymbiotic germination

Mature seed of most *Ophrys* species germinates relatively easily on a wide range of asymbiotic media, including Malmgren's, TGZ-SL or 25–50% Phytamax. 1% pineapple juice and swede (turnip) added at 4 ml per 100 ml (about 5 tsps/US pint) are complex additives proven by Malmgren to enhance germination. A sucrose concentration of 8–10 g/l (1.1–1.3 oz/US gallon) is best at this stage and all media must be pH adjusted to 5.5–6.0. *Ophrys insectifera* (like most *Orchis* and *Dactylorhiza* species) seems to germinate and grow better with 2% pineapple juice and potato rather than swede. Some species, particularly northern forms of *O. fuciflora*, somewhat surprisingly respond better to media that contains inorganic rather than organic nitrogen.

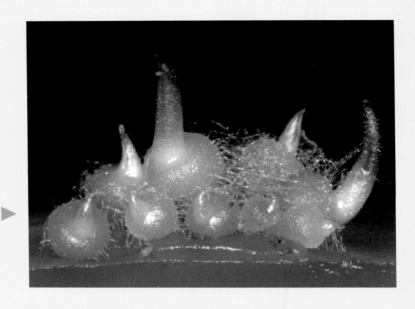

Protocorms of *Ophrys apifera* 4 weeks after germination

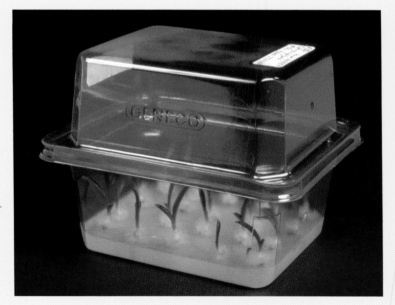

Well-spaced *Ophrys apifera* seedlings growing on a medium

Many growers recommend using dry seed that has been stored for two or three years in a refrigerator as it appears to germinate more easily than seed that has not been stored at low temperatures. The seed of southern species should be sown between February and April. Northern species, such as *O. apifera, O. insectifera* and some variants of *O. fuciflora* and *O. sphegodes*, are better sown in the autumn and then almost immediately placed in a refrigerator for 3 or 4 months over the winter. Return to room temperature in February or March so that the seeds will germinate in the spring. Seed usually needs to be sown two or three months before the seed capsules ripen in their natural habitats to allow asymbiotically grown protocorms to reach the correct stage of development for transfer into light conditions (whilst still *in vitro*) in the autumn.

Because seed can take many months to germinate when asymbiotic techniques are being used, flasks rather than Petri dishes are preferred for seed sowing.

Symbiotic germination

Many growers prefer to grow their plants symbiotically using a suitable fungus and an oat medium. Because symbiotic germination is relatively rapid, Petri dishes are ideal and symbiotic cultures of *Ophrys* seed will usually germinate at room temperature within 2 months. In this case, summer seed sowing should produce small plants with green leaves that can be potted up in late autumn of the same year.

The few available *Ophrys*-compatible fungi tend to lose their effectiveness with repeated sub-culture on oat medium and

are particularly slow-growing, facilitating infection of the cultures with unwanted organisms. Fungal associations in *Ophrys* are often species-specific and isolates rarely stimulate the germination of more than one or two species. Obtaining a culture of a fungus that is already stimulating the germination of the relevant orchid species is recommended.

Germination in the dark

Ophrys seed will only germinate in the dark. Flasks or Petri dishes should either be wrapped in foil, placed in a black plastic bag or placed at the back of a dark cupboard to keep the light out. With the exception of northern species, which often require refrigeration, the containers can be kept at room temperature until the seeds germinate.

Ophrys apifera with a new tuber beginning to form ▶

◀ **Symbiotic protocorms of Ophrys apifera**

Transplanting protocorms

Germination of all of the viable seeds is likely to take place over several months. As soon as a protocorm is large enough to be picked up, it should be transferred to fresh medium in a flask — leaving any remaining seeds to germinate and be transferred at a later date. If protocorms are not transplanted early in their development, they can rapidly form a tangled mat as their rhizoids begin to interweave. This makes them difficult or nigh on impossible to separate and inevitably many rhizoids will be damaged as the protocorms are teased apart.

Symbiotic protocorms will die if left on the sowing plate for too long. It is important to transplant them at a low density, with no more than 5–7 symbiotic protocorms to a flask or honey jar. Asymbiotic protocorms can be transplanted onto medium containing 12–15 g/l (0.2–0.25 oz/US pint) sucrose at two or three times the density recommended for symbiotic protocorms.

Once the first leaves begin to appear (this will be in the autumn if the seed has been sown at the correct time of year), the flasks of seedlings can be transferred to a cool and light location. Transferring to light too soon, or failure to cool at the correct stage, will kill the protocorms or young plants. It is essential that temperatures are kept low (8–12 °C/46–54 °F) over the winter months so that the young plants can grow properly. A gradual increase in spring-time temperatures will enhance the production of sinkers and tubers. Premature heat may kill the young plants by inducing early onset of dormancy before the tubers have been able to form properly.

Taller flasks such as honey jars (or Kilner jars) allow more headroom for the seedlings to grow. Remember that a medium that is suitable for germination may not necessarily be equally suitable for seedling growth. For *Ophrys* species (with the exception of *O. insectifera*), it is not recommended that pineapple juice should be incorporated into the growing medium because

▲ *Ophrys* **seedlings with tubers. It is important that the medium is sufficiently deep to prevent the sinkers pushing the seedlings up and out of the medium.**

it adversely affects root growth. According to Malmgren, swede remains an excellent complex organic additive for the growing medium. The sucrose concentration of the growing media can be usefully increased to 15 g/l (0.25 oz/US pint). The medium in the flask should also be deeper than that used for germination, allowing space for the sinker roots to grow down into the medium without pushing the seedlings up and out of the medium as they push against the bottom of the flask. These sinker roots will give rise to the first-year tubers. For optimum growth, plants growing *in vitro* should be transplanted onto fresh medium at least every 3 months. This requirement may vary according to the rate of growth, the density of plants in the flasks and whether or not the flasks are vented.

Transfer into compost

When the roots reach 1 cm (1/2") in length in late autumn or winter, symbiotic seedlings can be successfully weaned into compost (which may be heat-sterilised). The newly potted seedlings should then be kept over winter in a shady under-bench plunge bed in an unheated (cool but frost-free) greenhouse.

Asymbiotically grown plants should be maintained *in vitro* until their sinkers and tubers are well formed. Some growers wait until the foliage is browning and dying down before potting the now dormant tubers into dry soil or compost in the summer. Others consider it advantageous to wean the young plants into damp compost in the spring while they are still in growth and their tubers are still forming. Either way, Mediterranean species need to be dried off to some extent before their summer dormancy to avoid rotting. Northern species such as *O. apifera* do not take kindly to being over-dried and need some moisture at all times. *O. insectifera*, on the other hand, has a very short dormancy and positively dislikes being dried!

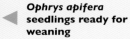

Ophrys apifera seedlings ready for weaning

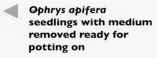

Ophrys apifera seedlings with medium removed ready for potting on

Plastic bottles can be used to prevent newly potted seedlings of *Ophrys apifera* from drying out

Everyone seems to have their own favourite recipe for compost. What is undeniable is that most *Ophrys* species grow naturally on chalk or limestone and thus prefer alkaline composts. If you live in an area that has chalky soil, you may be able to use your own garden soil as a compost component, otherwise you may choose to incorporate crushed limestone. The following compost mixes have been used successfully.

- Woodland loam collected from over hard limestone or chalk plus 20–40% sharp sand.

- Sieved chalky mole hills with added leaf mould and sharp sand.

- 2 parts limey loam, 3 parts beech leaf-mould, 1 part fine limestone chips, 2 parts fine horticultural grit, 2 parts coarse grit, and 1 part coarse Perlite.

Overwintering

Pots can be plunged in a bed of moist horticultural sand in a cold greenhouse or conservatory. The temperature should not be allowed to fall below 4 °C (39 °F) for species other than the hardy northern *O. apifera* and *O. insectifera* and high-latitude variants of *O. sphegodes* and *O. fuciflora*, which may be grown outside plunged in a cold frame. The compost should be constantly moist rather than wet, but should never be allowed to become at all dry during the growing period. Because of the low temperatures and high relative humidity at this time of year, there should be little need for watering, especially if plunged clay pots are used and the plunge material is kept wet. If you do have to water the compost, water carefully around the edge of the pot to avoid splashing water onto the leaves, or dampen the compost by partial plunging in water. Do not water at all in cold weather. If water does get onto the leaves, it can be soaked up with a piece of tissue or blown away using a drinking straw. Watering needs to be increased substantially in the spring before the leaves die down.

Inspect the plants regularly for aphids, which can infest your plants at any time of the year. If spotted early, they are easily removed with a moist soft paintbrush and can be disposed of appropriately.

Ophrys fusca

During the summertime

The leaves gradually die down in late spring or early summer as the plants enter their summer dormancy and the compost can be allowed to gradually dry out during this period. The degree to which the compost should be allowed to dry depends, to an extent, on the species of *Ophrys* in the pot. But even the most southern species should not be allowed to become desiccated. Once the compost has dried completely, a good method of preventing desiccation is to add back a small quantity of water (e.g. 50 ml (1.5 fl oz) for an 11 cm (4") clay pot) and then to seal the entire pot in a plastic bag and keep it in a dark place at room temperature until the autumn.

Alternatively, the tubers can be stored at ambient temperature over the summer in a plastic bag or plastic container (keep the tubers the right way up if possible) together with a little sand or dry vermiculite.

In the autumn

Tubers may be re-potted into fresh compost in the autumn but this is not necessary every year. Exposure to moisture (by watering) together with falling temperatures will make the tubers re-awaken.

Ophrys **tuber beginning to shoot** ▶

Young *Ophrys* plant growing in a plunged clay pot in the autumn
▼

◀ **Dry plants of *Ophrys* ready for their summer rest**

Cypripedium

Cypripedium species are generally considered more challenging than most other terrestrial orchids in terms of their willingness to germinate and the ease with which they can be raised *in vitro* and grown in pots or in the garden. Successful cultivation of these most desirable but sometimes demanding plants, with their often stunningly beautiful flowers, is considered by many to be the apex of horticultural excellence.

Cypripedium is a genus of about 50 species that are adapted to the temperate and sub-tropical alpine climates of the northern hemisphere. These orchids are widespread throughout Europe, temperate Asia, China, Japan and North America. They are terrestrial herbs, with a short to creeping rhizome and a fibrous root system. Their thin leaves cannot withstand high temperatures and low humidity.

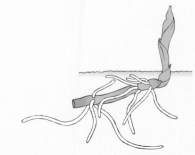

Cypripedium **Lucy Pinkepank**

Life cycle of *Cypripedium macranthos*

The lifecycle of *Cypripedium macranthos* is typical of that of other members of the genus. The species is distributed from eastern-most Europe across most of northern Asia to the Pacific Ocean. The populations found in the mountains north of Beijing are at the south-eastern boundary of the general distribution. There, *C. macranthos* is found together with *C. guttatum* at an altitude of up to 2,000 m above sea level in sub-alpine meadows or, where the light is adequate, under birch canopies. *C. macranthos* grows in humus-rich soil with a pH of 6–7. Its growing period is short: around 5 months.

Naturally occurring populations of *C. macranthos* typically consist of several clumps comprised of single- or few-shooted specimens. Under favourable conditions, individual clones can develop many shoots clustered together in a more or less dense clump.

In most of the distribution range of *C. macranthos*, the winters are consistently

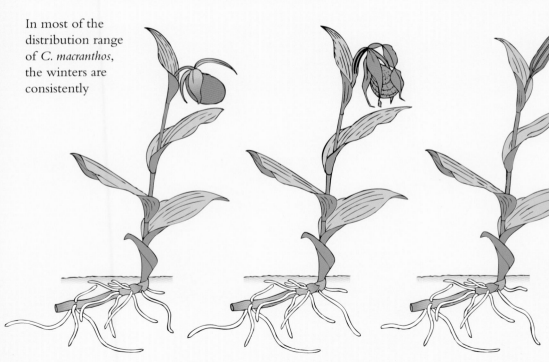

chilly and dry. This is in contrast to western and central European winters, which are typically wet and include spells of warm weather. Therefore, some winter protection from excess water is essential. The summers experienced by *C. macranthos* growing in its natural environment are cool and rainy. Plants in cultivation in regions that have dry hot summers therefore require a lot of watering and protection from direct sunlight.

May

The above-ground parts of the plants begin to emerge in May as the soil temperatures at root level gradually warm and the frozen ground begins to thaw.

June

The plants bloom in June for about 3 weeks in total. The average individual flowers last around 9 days without pollination, and 2 or 3 days less if pollinated. Bumblebees are the most common pollinators of both wild and cultivated populations around Beijing. Both cross-pollination and self-pollination of *C. macranthos* produces viable seed.

September

The leaves and stems turn brown and gradually die down in the autumn. Seed capsules ripen from mid to late September.

October

Normally, the flower buds for the next blooming season will have completed their development during the summer. The rhizome and growth buds become dormant as soil temperatures fall below zero.

Asymbiotic germination

Immature seed

Obtaining successful germination of *Cypripedium* seed on artificial media can be challenging, with mature seed generally being considered more difficult to germinate than immature seed. However, immature seed can be difficult to obtain. Mature seed will remain viable for several years if dried and stored in a sealed container in a refrigerator at 4–5 °C (39–41 °F).

Because of the potential problems involved in breaking the seed dormancy of *Cypripedium* species, many (perhaps the majority) of growers prefer to sow immature seed. The capsules can be harvested between 5 and 12 weeks after pollination, depending on the species and climatic conditions.

The seeds should be sown on Petri dishes using the 'green pod' method. (The whole capsule is first surface-sterilised in bleach then dipped in alcohol and passed briefly through a flame. Under sterile conditions, it is then cut open and the seeds spread on the surface.) The plates should them be placed in the dark at room temperature (18–20 °C/4–68 °F). Germination, which generally occurs after about 10–12 weeks, results in embryo swelling and the production of a smooth white protocorm with no rhizoids.

Cypripedium calceolus germinates well on Malmgren's medium. In order to encourage root growth rather than shoot growth, the jars should remain in the dark until the plants are large enough for vernalisation. An occasional short exposure to light when checking plants will not cause too much damage, but longer periods of light exposure will cause the shoots to elongate and turn green or black and root growth to cease. Some growers have reported that the protocorms of some *Cypripedium* species die when subjected to even short periods of daylight. Thus, some growers recommend examining plants under green light only.

Mature seed

As with other genera, the seeds of some *Cypripedium* species are easier to germinate than those of others. We suggest that you start out with seed that is relatively easy to germinate such as that of hybrids or of species such as *C. acaule*, *C. californicum*, *C. flavum*, *C. guttatum*, *C. parviflorum* and *C. reginae*. Ideally, seed should be harvested just prior to the splitting of the seed capsule.

Mature *Cypripedium* seed is comparatively difficult to germinate because the ripening processes that lead to its dormancy take place within the capsule in the final few weeks before the capsule splits in the autumn. The seed will naturally remain dormant in the soil over the winter months and germinate the following spring. Often (but not always) the seeds require a cold winter before they can break dormancy and germinate. These natural conditions can be replicated by storing the seeds in a refrigerator at a temperature just above freezing for a minimum of two, but preferably four, months. Alternatively, in culture, seed dormancy can sometimes be broken successfully by using plant hormones or extended bleaching times.

Germinating seeds of *Cypripedium plectrochilum*. The embryos can be clearly seen bursting through the tough inner carapace characteristic of *Cypripedium* seeds.

Seed sterilisation is important

The sterilisation of *Cypripedium* seed usually requires amendments to the standard orchid procedures described in *Growing Orchids from Seed* to ensure successful germination. *Cypripedium* seed may require much longer sterilisation periods than those commonly used for other orchid species because the bleaching processes involved in sterilisation help to break the dormancy of *Cypripedium* seed. The deep dormancy of *Cypripedium* seeds is largely due to the physical barrier formed by their inner seed coat (or carapace). This can be overcome by chemically corroding the layers of lignin and suberin in the carapace, especially in the region of the embryo suspensor.

The correct bleaching time depends on the species, the concentration of the bleach solution, the ratio between bleach volume and seed mass, and the temperature of the bleach. *C. macranthos*, for example, often germinates well when bleached for 40 minutes in 0.5% sodium hypochlorite solution. Even within a species, variations in bleaching requirements can be associated with the provenance of the seed and the density of the carapace, and requirements can differ from year to year. The best advice we can offer is that growers should observe the seeds carefully during the bleaching process, and should stop this process when the embryos have reached a pale yellow honey colour. This is easy to detect in species with dark embryos but difficult to see in species whose embryos are initially very pale.

In conclusion, most fully ripe and dry *Cypripedium* seeds will germinate only when the bleaching protocol is sufficiently vigorous to open up the carapace, and perhaps inactivate dormancy factors in the embryo cells close to the embryo suspensor by killing these cells. Simply surface-sterilising seeds and keeping them refrigerated for two or three months on the germination medium often gives only poor and erratic germination.

Cypripedium calceolus seedlings growing on a medium that contains charcoal ▶

◀ **Cypripedium calceolus seeds and protocorms**

Germination media

Mature seeds of *C. acaule*, *C. parviflorum* var. *parviflorum*, *C. parviflorum* var. *pubescens* and *C. reginae* have all been found to germinate well on one-third strength Murashige & Skoog medium with the addition of 100 ml/l coconut water, 15 g/l sucrose and 7 g/l agar. This medium must be adjusted to pH 6 before being sterilised by autoclaving. Some authors recommend germinating seed in liquid suspension culture, finding it quicker than using solid media, and having the advantage of making it easier to separate seedlings for transplanting. A disadvantage of the liquid suspension technique, however, is that it does require an orbital shaker. Some *Cypripedium* species, such as *C. kentuckiense*, can be intolerant of the ammonium ion, which appears to inhibit their growth after germination. A medium with organic nitrogen (casein hydrolysate) might therefore be more suitable for transfer after germination. Malmgren's medium has amino acids as its nitrogen source and is excellent for many cypripediums.

Cypripedium seed must be incubated in the dark and at room temperature (around 21 °C/70 °F). Chilling at 5 °C/41 °F for 8 weeks after sowing can enhance the germination of some species.

As the seeds germinate, the dark brown carapace ruptures and a pearly white embryo emerges. Germination generally occurs after about 10–12 weeks, although some species take much longer. The embryo is gradually transformed into a smooth white protocorm (often without rhizoids) which proceeds to form one or two long roots. Protocorms should be transferred to fresh medium in larger vessels before the first root elongates beyond 2 cm (1") to prevent roots intertwining, browning and becoming damaged on transfer.

The following autumn, the seedlings should be chilled for a second time. *Cypripedium* seedlings will not produce leaves unless they receive a second cold treatment by placing them in a refrigerator at about 4 °C/39 °F for at least 3 months.

◄ **Cypripedium yunnanense**

Micropropagated Cypripedium seedlings in zip lock bags ▶

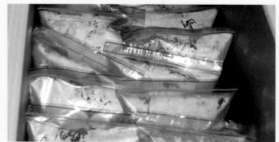

Micropropagated Cypripedium seedlings in fridge ▶

Symbiotic germination

Mycorrhizal fungi that are compatible with *Cypripedium* species are not currently available for purchase, but in the past few years symbiotic fungi that are suitable for the germination of a few *Cypripedium* species have been isolated. *C. macranthos* in China and *C. formosanum* in Taiwan have been successfully germinated using a symbiotic fungus.

Transplanting the protocorms

When the protocoms are approximately 5 mm in diameter and triangular in shape, having formed an initial shoot plus 2 root initials, they can be transferred to fresh medium in larger vessels.

The roots can be easily damaged during the transfer as they are brittle. So rather than frequent transfer, it may be preferable to space the protocorms generously (1 seedling per 10 ml medium) on media with relatively low agar concentration of 5 g/l or even less, depending on the quality of the agar. Some growers prefer 1.5 g/l gellan gum (available as Gelrite or Phytagel™) to enable the penetration of roots into the medium as they grow. A greater depth of medium will allow the plants to be nourished throughout their time in culture and it may not be necessary to transfer them to flasks of fresh medium. If transfer is necessary, damage to the brittle roots in re-establishing the plants in new medium can be minimised by pouring cool, sterile media that has not yet solidified into the sterile vessels containing the transferred seedlings. The cooling media will solidify around the root systems and will avoid further damage that might occur when trying to push root systems into solidified media.

Seedling vernalisation

When possible, a sterile refrigeration unit in a clean room can provide a space in which to vernalise smaller seedlings *in vitro*. Flasks can be placed into plastic storage bags and stacked into the chiller to simulate the normal winter dormancy. Alternatively, plants that are large enough for potting up can be placed in a fridge (0–4 °C/32–39 °F) over winter before being transplanted into compost in the spring. The plants are removed from the jars, taking care not to damage the roots (which may be up to 30 cm long) (a process much facilitated by using gellan gum in the medium), rinsed in sterile water to remove any remaining gelling agent and sealed in thick polythene bags. The bags take up less space than storage jars and can be easily transported or posted.

Cypripedium calceolus in fridge ▶

Cypripedium calceolus potted up in the spring, placed in a cold frame and plunged in horticultural sand ▶

Cypripedium in the greenhouse and garden

We suggest that growers who are new to raising *Cypripedium* from seed should initially choose the less expensive hybrids and cut their growing teeth on plants that are relatively easy to grow. Nursery staff should be able to assist in this choice.

In the greenhouse or cold frame

When potting up seedlings, place the growth bud at or just below the surface of the compost and spread out the roots evenly to encourage them to grow down into the compost. After placing plenty of drainage material in the bottom of the pot, make a mound of compost and place the growth bud on top. Back-fill the pot with more compost and top dress with a free-draining material such as grit (which can also help to deter slugs). Cypripediums are shallow-rooted and can be grown in half-pans.

Many compost mixtures have been tried, from soil taken from sites similar to those where the orchids grow naturally (but not from the actual site) to artificial mixes containing perlite or Seramis®. Organic material should not be included in the compost. In nature, most *Cypripedium* species grow in free-draining soils in areas of relatively high humidity, and you should aim to replicate these conditions as far as possible. Composts should be free-draining but moisture-retentive. Cypripediums resent drying out and will quickly die if moisture is absent from the compost. On the other hand, the compost should not be wet. To avoid rotting of the rhizomes, especially during the winter, water around the edge of the pot.

Cypripediums are not heavy feeders: during the growing period, water them occasionally with any general garden fertiliser diluted to half normal strength.

▲ *Cypripedium* seedlings (Year 1)

▲ *Cypripedium* seedlings (Year 2)

▲ *Cypripedium* seedlings (Year 3)

In the garden

As an alternative to greenhouse culture, plants can be overwintered by burying the pot in the garden soil in a shady spot. This will help to maintain a stable temperature and, unless the soil is very dry, will maintain evenly moist conditions. Although the plants will normally survive low winter temperatures, they do resent being wet. Pots can be covered with a tile, a sheet of glass or a cloche to prevent the compost becoming too wet during periods of heavy rain. One advantage of using a cloche is that it also provides protection from slugs and snails.

Cypripedium can be grown successfully in the garden, but it may be necessary to prepare a special bed for them first. They usually grow in dappled shade and too much sunlight will burn the thin leaves. Large clumps should be divided.

Some *Cypripedium* species require very specialised conditions. For example, the beautiful pink-flowered North American species *C. acaule* (moccasin orchid) grows in pine woods and requires an acidic soil. To ensure the long-term survival of these plants in the garden, they should be watered regularly with 30 ml cider vinegar per 3.8 litres of distilled water (roughly 1 tsp/US pint) as the substrate must not have a pH higher than 4–4.5 at any time.

Cypripedium parviflorum var. pubescens

Pleione

Pleione **Versailles**

Originating in the cool moist habitats of the mountains of eastern Asia these charming orchids usually flower in the spring. Frequently grown in half-pans in a frost-free greenhouse, they can make a spectacular sight when several bulbs of one species or hybrid are flowering at the same time. Sometimes referred to as 'windowsill orchids', flowering specimens can also be enjoyed indoors. However, as long as they are protected from winter frosts several species and many lovely hybrids with long-lasting flowers are relatively hardy and will survive outside in sheltered and well-drained conditions.

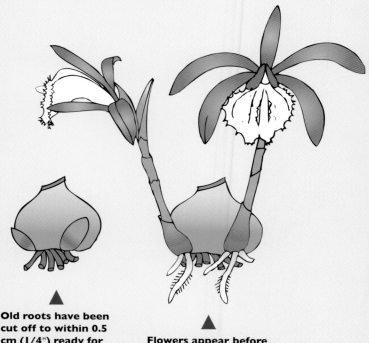

▲ **Old roots have been cut off to within 0.5 cm (1/4") ready for repotting**

▲ **Flowers appear before the leaves in spring**

Life cycle of a hardy *Pleione*

March

New stems and/or flower buds begin to appear. Flowers form on 15–20 cm (6–8") stems. New leaves begin to emerge when flowering has finished.

April and May

Once the flowers begin to fade, the shoots develop rapidly into large thin pleated leaves about 15 cm (6") long and 5 cm (2") wide. The pseudobulbs begin to show signs of shrivelling as their reserves are consumed.

June to August

The new shoots begin to fatten at their bases and the new pseudobulbs begin to develop.

September and October

By now, the pseudobulbs are plump, the leaves begin to show increasing signs of ageing and are eventually shed. By late September, growth has more or less ceased for the season and the pseudobulbs enter their winter rest period. The roots stop growing about three weeks after leaf fall.

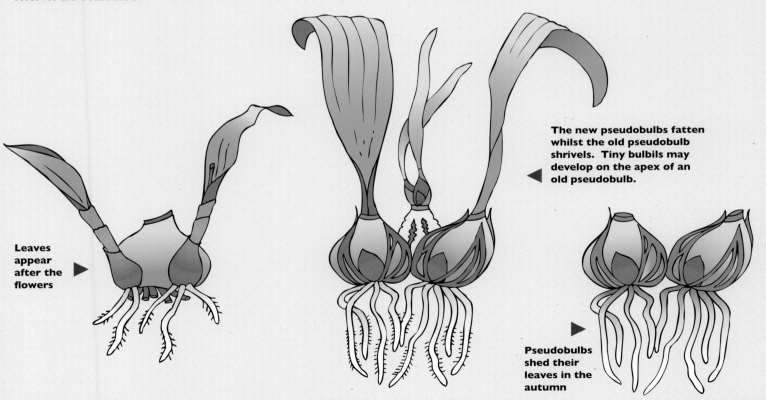

The new pseudobulbs fatten whilst the old pseudobulb shrivels. Tiny bulbils may develop on the apex of an old pseudobulb.

Leaves appear after the flowers ▶

Pseudobulbs shed their leaves in the autumn

Buying pleiones

Ready-potted pseudobulbs can be purchased in the spring, either in bud or in flower. Alternatively, you can buy pseudobulbs of flowering size from late autumn until the end of February to pot up yourself. Examine the pseudobulbs carefully. Generally speaking, the bigger the pseudobulb the better. Larger pseudobulbs can have two or even three flower buds, which in turn also means that, if well-grown, they are capable of producing two or three flowering-size pseudobulbs by the autumn.

Potting

Pleiones should be re-potted each spring before they come into flower and before any new roots begin to emerge. Any dead roots should be trimmed to within 0.5 cm (1/4") of the pseudobulb. You may also wish to remove the dead bracts, although it might be wiser to leave them in place as it is very easy to damage developing flower buds accidentally during the process of removing the bracts.

Pleiones are relatively shallow-rooted, and groups can be cultivated in a frost-free greenhouse in trays or 'half-height' pots. The pseudobulbs do well when planted closely together, allowing about 1 cm (1/2") between each (for large pseudobulbs). Bury the pseudobulbs so that one-third is still visible above the compost and place the pots in cool but frost-free conditions. Annual re-potting is good horticultural practice and provides an opportunity to inspect the pseudobulbs for pests such as false spider mites and their eggs; if necessary, the pseudobulbs can be cleaned or treated with an insecticide.

Composts

Use a compost that is open and free-draining but relatively water-retentive. A mixture of pine bark, sphagnum moss (for moisture retention), Perlite and perhaps a little oak or beech leaf mould makes a suitable compost.

Watering

As the flower buds begin to develop, you should be very circumspect about watering. Although the compost should be slightly moist and not bone-dry, no additional water should be given until the roots begin to appear. In the spring, the compost should be moist rather than wet. Over-watering at this time can soon lead to the death of new roots. Because pleiones only produce one flush of roots in the spring, root death caused by waterlogging can be disastrous.

In late spring, as the plants build up a strong root system, watering can gradually be increased and feeding can begin. It is usually better to water in the morning so that the leaves are dry by nightfall; but on warm summer days, watering in the evening is preferred as a moist night-time atmosphere helps the plants to recover from heat stress. Watering should be gradually reduced throughout the late summer and into autumn.

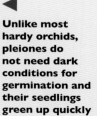

Unlike most hardy orchids, pleiones do not need dark conditions for germination and their seedlings green up quickly

Feeding

All feed should be applied at half the recommended strength. The addition of too much phosphate in the compost can lead to browning of the ends of the leaves. A balanced feed with an NPK ratio of 30:30:30 should be applied on a regular basis in the early part of the growing season. Towards the end of the summer, this can be replaced with feed that has a higher ratio of phosphorus and potassium, such as a tomato fertiliser.

During the summertime

Pleione plants can be can be taken outside after the last frosts (around the middle of May) and placed in a shady location. Flower buds and young leaves are tender and, whether growing outdoors or under glass, they must be shaded from strong sunlight in order to prevent scorching. Too much moisture will almost certainly kill these plants and thus the choice of soil and location is crucial: good drainage can be ensured by planting on a slope, in a raised bed or in the vertical cracks of a peat wall, or by adding plenty of grit to the soil.

Overwintering

Plants that are to be overwintered indoors should be brought into a cool, frost-free greenhouse or into the house before the first autumn frosts. Dormant pseudobulbs can also be stored in sealed plastic bags in a cool, dry place for at least 6–8 weeks (November to January) so that their vernalisation is completed. Temperatures of 3–5 °C (37–41 °F) are ideal, and can be achieved by placing the pseudobulbs in the bottom of a refrigerator.

If left outdoors, it is advisable to protect the pseudobulbs against rain during the winter either by placing a sheet of glass over them or by planting them under shrubs such as camellias or rhododendrons. Sites that have early-morning sun in winter should be avoided as the plants will not tolerate being regularly frozen and thawed.

Not all pleiones are spring-flowering. Autumn-flowering Himalayan species such as *Pleione praecox* (shown here) and *P. maculata* flower after they have shed their leaves before entering their winter dormancy.

Hardy orchid genera

Galearis roborowskii

ACERAS
man orchid

Monotypic European and Mediterranean genus. Placed in *Orchis* by some authors.

Recommended
A. anthropophorum, commonly called man orchid because of the shape of the lip which resembles a hanging man.

Hybrids *Orchiaceras* × *bergonii* (with *Orchis simia*), *O.* × *duhartii* (with *O. purpurea*), and *O.* × *spuria* (with *O. militaris*) are attractive natural hybrids.

Habitat Chalk and limestone grassland and scrub.

Culture Garden.

Compost A.

Aceras anthropophorum

AMITOSTIGMA

27 species from China, Korea and Japan.

Recommended *A. lepidum* from Okinawa; *A. tibeticum* and *A. monanthum* both from western China and Tibet.

Habitat Alpine rocks and grassland, shady banks.

Culture Cool greenhouse or cold frame.

Compost A.

Amitostigma monanthum

ANACAMPTIS

11 species in Europe and the Mediterranean. Several species were formerly ascribed to *Orchis*.

Recommended *Anacamptis pyramidalis* (pyramidal orchid), *A. morio* (green-winged orchid), *A. laxiflora* (lax-flowered orchid), *A. coriophora* (bug orchid) and *A. papilionacea* (butterfly orchid).

Habitat Dry grassland and scrub, damp grassland and marsh.

Culture Garden or cool greenhouse. *A. morio*, *A. laxiflora* and *A. pyramidalis* can be naturalised.

Compost A.

Anacamptis morio

BARLIA
giant orchid

Two species from the the Mediterranean and the Canary Islands. Included in *Himantoglossum* by some authors.

Recommended *B. robertiana* and *B. metlesicsiana*.

Habitat Grassland and scrub on limestone.

Culture Frost-free greenhouse. Flowers early in the year, often in February.

Compost B.

Barlia robertiana

BLETILLA
hyacinth orchid

Four or five species from the Far East.

Recommended *B. striata* (hyacinth orchid), an important plant in Chinese traditional medicine (called 'Bai ji'). A form with white flowers and another with variegated leaves are not uncommon in cultivation. *B. formosana* is a more delicate species. *B. ochracea* has yellow flowers that rival those of *B. striata* in size.

Hybrids *B.* Brigantes (*B. striata* × *B. ochracea*), *B.* Coritani (*B. formosana* × *B. ochracea*) and *B.* Yokohama (*B. striata* × *B. formosana*).

Habitat Rocky hillsides, in mountains and hills, and at forest margins.

Culture Garden or cool greenhouse. Both *B. striata* and *B. ochracea* are hardy to at least USDA zone 5 and have survived into zone 6.5.

Compost D.

Bletilla striata

CALADENIA
spider orchids

Over 260 species, mostly from south-east and south-western Australia but a few species are also found in New Zealand, New Guinea, Timor and Java. Known as spider orchids because a number of species have spidery flowers with long tapering sepals and petals.

Recommended *C. menziesii, C. latifolia, C. carnea, C. catenata, C. dilatata. C. menziesii, C. latifolia* and *C. cairnsiana* multiply vegetatively. Most, such as *C. carnea, C. dilatata, C. flava* and *C. patersonii*, can only be grown from seed. Many species are difficult to grow in cultivation. The blue-flowered species, including *C. deformis* and *C. gemmata*, have been transferred to the genus *Cyanicula*.

Habitat Marshes, sandy plains, scrub and woodland on acidic soils.

Culture Some are suitable for pot culture in a frost-free glasshouse.

Compost F.

Caladenia flava

Caladenia deformis

Caladenia flava

CALANTHE

About 200 species, widespread in the Old World tropics and subtropics but extending to Tahiti in the Pacific Ocean and with a single species in the tropical Americas. Only the species from Japan, China, Korea and the Himalayas are at all hardy.

Recommended *C. discolor* from China, Korea and Japan; the similar but paler-flowered *C. izu-insularis*; the canary yellow *C. striata* (syn. *C. sieboldii*) from Japan and China; *C. tricarinata* from the Himalayas, China, Japan and Korea; and *C. graciliflora* from China and Taiwan.

Hybrids *C.* Takane (*C. discolor* × *C. striata*) and *C.* Satsuma (*C. striata* × *C. aristulifera*). The hybrids are rather larger and more vigorous plants and are available in a wide variety of flower colours. They are traditionally grown and shown in elegant pots in the Far East where their cultivation is a major hobby.

Habitat Mostly woodland species in deep shade.

Culture Garden or cool greenhouse. Pans can be grown under the bench in a glasshouse or elsewhere in deep shade. Calanthes can be grown in shady places in the garden, provided that they are protected from cold, damp conditions in winter.

Compost D.

Calanthe izu-insularis

Calanthe tricarinata

Calanthe striata

CALOPOGON
grass pink

Five similar species from the United States, all bar one restricted to the south-eastern states.

Recommended *C. tuberosus* and *C. pulchellus*.

Habitat Marshes and open swamps.

Culture Cool greenhouse.

Compost G.

Calopogon tuberosus

CEPHALANTHERA
helleborine orchids

A circumboreal genus of about 20 species.

Recommended The European *C. damasonium*, *C. longifolia* and *C. rubra*; *C. falcata* from East Asia.

Habitat Woodlands in deep to light shade.

Culture Gardens. Sometimes found naturally in gardens under trees, especially in chalk and limestone soils.

Compost C.

Cephalanthera longifolia

CHLORAEA

52 species mainly from Chile and Argentina. Related to other South American terrestrials, such as *Bipinnula*, *Codonorchis* and *Gavilea*.

Recommended *C. chrysantha*, *C. gavilu*, *C. lechleri* and *C. virescens*.

Hybrids Using *C. crispa*, artificial infra- and inter-specific hybrids with yellow or pale brown flowers have been produced.

Habitat Two main groups can be recognised:

A. Those from a Mediterranean–like environment, with a cool, wet winter, a dry, hot summer and poor, mostly weathered granite soils. *C incisa*, *C. virescens*, *C. chrysantha*, *C. gavilu* and *C. lechleri* grow in shaded places. *C. cylindrostachya*, *C. leptopetala*, *C. magellanica* and *C. virescens* are found on eroded volcanic sand. *C. bletioides* grows in richer soils in the shade of native bamboo. A compost that is low in organic material is recommended: for example, 30% Perlite, 30% Seramis®, 30% lava grit and 10% fine-grade bark. A minimum temperature of 3 °C (37 °F) is recommended.

B. *C. magellanica* and *C. leptopetala* grow in dry and cold steppe-like climates, such as those of southern Chile and Argentina. There, precipitation is low and conditions are windy, but temperatures do not fluctuate much throughout the year. Day-time temperatures are mostly below 10 °C (50 °F) during the summer and above 2 °C (36 °F) in the winter.

Chloraea virescens

Culture Frost-free greenhouse. These winter-green species produce a rosette or growth from which an inflorescence is sent up in spring. Pollination occurs in late spring.

Compost I. Chloraeas need a lime-free sandy or gritty compost and space in the pots for their fleshy roots to spread. They have tap roots that are easily damaged, and therefore should be potted into deep pots.

Chloraea bletioides

COELOGLOSSUM
frog orchids

A monotypic, circumboreal genus. DNA analysis has shown that the genus is sister to *Dactylorhiza*, and some botanists include it there.

Recommended *C. viride*.

Habitat Grassland, scrub and woodland on limestone and neutral soils.

Culture Some *Coeloglossum* species are easy to grow if transplanted into a garden, provided that the soils have not been enriched with nutrients. Most European species can be naturalised.

Compost B.

Coeloglossum viride

CORYBAS
helmet orchids

A large genus distributed from China and the Himalayas through the mountains of South-east Asia and the Malay Archipelago to Australia, Tasmania and New Zealand.

Recommended Only the southern Australasian species tolerate lower temperatures and can be grown in a cool glasshouse. Easily grown species include *C. aconitiflorus*, *C. diemenicus*, *C. fimbriatus*, *C. hispidus*, *C. incurvus*, *C. orbicularis* and *C. pruinosus*.

Habitat Woodland and open areas on acidic sandy soils.

Culture Cool greenhouse. Humidity around the plants can be maintained using a bell-jar to ensure that these plants do not dry out between waterings.

Compost F. Should be re-potted annually.

Corybas orbicularis

Cymbidium
goeringii

CYMBIDIUM

About 50 species, from subtropical regions in Asia and Australia as far north as Korea and Japan. A favourite genus of the Chinese since the time of Confucius (551–479 BC), cymbidiums are often grown in the Far East in pots in courtyards, around temples, on balconies and in traditional orchid gardens.

Recommended The hardiest species is *C. goeringii* from China, Korea and Japan. Cultivated plants, which have been selected over generations for features such as variegated leaves and distorted or unusually coloured flowers, are greatly valued and can fetch high prices in the Far East. The spring-flowering *C. faberi*; the autumn-flowering *C. ensifolium* and *C. kanran*; and the autumn- and winter-flowering *C. sinense* are also recommended.

Habitat Mostly in woodland shade on humus-rich soils.

Culture *C. goeringii* can be grown outside in southern Britain if given some protection from winter cold and damp; the rest need a cool greenhouse.

Compost D.

*Cymbidium
ensifolium*

CYPRIPEDIUM
hardy slipper orchids, lady's slipper orchids

50 species, circumboreal, 32 species in temperate China and 12 species in North America.

Recommended Pink- to purple-flowered species: *C. reginae* from North America, *C. macranthos* (from eastern Europe across northern Asia to Japan, China and Taiwan), *C. tibeticum* (from the Himalayas and western China), *C. calcicola*, *C. franchetii* and *C. yunnanense* (all from western China), *C. formosanum* (from Taiwan) and *C. japonicum* (from Japan and China).

Yellow-flowered species: *C. flavum* (from western China), *C. parviflorum* var. *parviflorum* and var. *pubescens* (from North America) and *C. kentuckiense* (from central-southern USA).

The Eurasian *C. calceolus* is less easy to grow than *C. parviflorum*. The Chinese *C. henryi* is similar to *C. calceolus* but usually has two or three green flowers on each stem; the Taiwanese *C. segawai* is similar but its single flower is yellow. *C. fasciolatum* has a flower that resembles a very large *C. calceolus* flower but with much longer yellow sepals and petals, which often have red-brown streaks, and a lip of about 5 cm x 3 cm (2" x 1 1/4"). *C. farreri* is smaller but the lip is fluted towards the mouth and toothed along the rim.

White-flowered species: *C. californicum* (from California and southern Oregon), *C. montanum* (from western North America) and *C. candidum* (from the prairies of North America). The Chinese *C. plectrochilum* and the North America *C. arietinum* are called ram's head slipper orchids because of their distinctive pointed hairy lip.

Spotted-leaved species: the Chinese *C. margaritaceum*, *C. fargesii*, *C. lichiangense* and *C. lentiginosum*.

Dwarf species: *C. guttatum*, *C. debile* and *C. palangshanensene*.

Cypripedium parviflorum var. pubescens

Cypripedium formosanum

Cypripedium californicum

Hybrids We recommend that you cut your growing teeth on hybrids as they are easier to grow than *Cypripedium* species.

Yellow-flowered hybrids: *C.* Emil (*C. parviflorum* × *C. calceolus*) and *C.* Hank Small (*C. parviflorum* × *C. henryi*) have flowers that resemble small *C. calceolus* flowers, but these hybrids are much easier to grow and bring into flower; *C.* Inge (*C. parviflorum* × *C. fasciolatum*) and *C.* Victoria (*C. parviflorum* var. *pubescens* × *C. fasciolatum*) are, respectively, hybrids of *C. parviflorum* var. *parviflorum* and var. *pubescens* with *C. fasciolatum*. They both have the large flowers of the pollen parent.

Pink- or purple-flowered hybrids: *C.* × *ventricosum* (*C. calceolus* × *C. macranthos*), *C.* Sabine (*C. fasciolatum* × *C. macranthos*), *C.* Philipp (*C. macranthos* × *C. kentuckiense*) and *C.* Michael (*C. macranthos* × *C. henryi*). *C.* Ulla Silkens, a hybrid of *C. reginae* and *C. flavum*, has whitish to pale purple flowers with a red-spotted lip. It is easier to grow than either parent and is very similar in colour to *C. reginae*.

Habitat Forest and woodland margins or glades, grassland, meadows and among ferns. Rarely in acidic woods; sea level to 4,000 m.

Culture Cool greenhouses or cold frames or gardens.

Compost C. *C. acaule* requires specialised conditions and should be watered regularly with 30 ml cider vinegar in 3.8 litres of distilled water (roughly 1 tsp/US pint): the substrate must not have a pH higher than 4–4.5.

Cypripedium hybrids

Cypripedium fasciolatum

DACTYLORHIZA
spotted and marsh orchids

Some 40 species in Europe and Asia and one species, *D. aristata*, native to North America. Many species are morphologically variable; others, such as *D. incarnata* and *D. fuchsii*, are tetraploids.

Recommended *D. fuchsii* (heath spotted orchid), *D. maculata*, *D. praetermissa* (southern marsh orchid), *D. purpurella* (from northern Europe), the yellow- or purple-flowered *D. sambucina* (from the mountains of Europe), *D. elata* (from south-western Europe) and the Madeiran endemic, *D. foliosa*.

Hybrids *D. × grandis* (*D. fuchsii* × *D. praetermissa*).

Habitat Meadows, grassland on limestone and marshes. *D. fuchsii*, *D. maculata* and *D. praetermissa* are sometimes found in lawns and grassy areas in gardens where no fertilisers have been used.

Culture Some *Dactylorhiza* species are easy to grow if transplanted into a garden, provided that the soils have not been enriched with nutrients. Most European species can be naturalised.

Compost B. Most species and hybrids are damp-loving and need well-drained but water-retentive compost that has a relatively high organic content. A couple of suggestions that have been used with some success are: **A.** 4 parts composted bark, 1 part loam, 2 parts coarse Perlite and 2 parts sharp sand; or **B.** 3 parts milled peat, 1 part loam, 1 part grit and 2 parts sharp sand. Other growers have used composts that have a low organic content with success, but these require very frequent use of fertilisers for good growth. One such compost is: 6 parts Seramis®, 5 parts coarse Perlite, 5 parts vermiculite, 1 part loam and 1 part fine orchid bark.

Dactylorhiza foliosa

Dactylorhiza foliosa

Dactylorhiza elata

DACTYLOSTALIX

A monotypic genus from Japan.

Recommended *D. ringens*.

Habitat In small colonies in leaf litter on the forest floor.

Culture Cool greenhouse; it is grown as a pot plant in Japan.

Compost D.

Dactylostalix ringens

DENDROBIUM

About 1,000 species distributed throughout tropical and subtropical Asia to Australia and the Pacific islands.

Recommended Only one species, the Japanese and Chinese *D. moniliforme*. 'Tananishiki', a form with variegated leaves from Japan, and 'Kyomarubotan', a form with marginally variegated leaves, are often available in specialised nurseries.

Habitat Epiphytic or lithoplytic in woodland forest.

Culture Cool greenhouse. *D. moniliforme* will tolerate winter cold but not winter dampness, and it needs some protection from the latter.

Compost H.

Dendrobium moniliforme

DISA

178 species confined to Africa and Madagascar. Only the South African species are at all hardy.

Recommended *D. cardinalis* and *D. uniflora*, the 'pride of Table Mountain', which is the provincial flower of Cape Province. *D. aurata* has been used to produce yellow-flowered hybrids, whereas *D. tripetaloides* has been used to produce pink-flowered hybrids.

Hybrids Many, including *D.* Watsonii, *D.* Kewensis and *D.* Kirstenbosch Pride.

Habitat *D. uniflora* grows on the banks of fast-flowing streams on Table Mountain and some of the nearby ranges.

Culture Frost-free greenhouse.

Compost G. Also open lime-free composts or lime-free sand.

Disa uniflora

Disa aurata

DIURIS
donkey orchids

50 or more species in Australia. Known as donkey orchids because of their usually erect spathulate petals, which rise above the flower.

Recommended Yellow-flowered species: *D. longifolia*, *D. behrii* (endemic to South Australia), *D. corymbosa*, *D. maculata* (from coastal New South Wales), *D. magnifica* (from Western Australia) and the lemon-yellow-flowered *D. sulphurea*.

Purple-flowered species: *D. punctata*. The beautiful *D. fragrantissima* from Victoria is greatly endangered in the wild but has been cultivated successfully.

Habitat Can form extensive colonies in favourable open habitats on open sandy soils and in grassland.

Culture Frost-free greenhouse, in full sun.

Compost F.

*Diuris
pardina*

Diuris fragrantissima

EPIPACTIS helleborines

About 50 species, circumboreal.

Recommended *E. helleborine* (broad-leaved helleborine) and *E. palustris* (marsh helleborine) from Europe and Asia, *E. gigantea* from the western USA, *E. veratrifolia* from the Middle East and north-eastern Africa, *E. mairei* from western China and the eastern Himalayas, the Himalayan species *E. royleana*, and *E. thunbergii* and *E. xanthophaea* from Japan, Korea and China.

Hybrids *E.* Sabine. More hybrids of *E. gigantea*, *E. veratrifolia*, *E. mairei* and *E. royleana*, in various combinations, are beginning to appear on the market. They are vigorous plants that are likely to be easier to grow than their parents.

Habitat *E. gigantea*, which grows in wet flushes and by streams in arid areas of the American West, is a good garden plant, thriving on the margins of ponds or in permanently wet marshy areas. It produces orange-brown flowers of more than 1 cm across. The fine cultivar 'Serpentine Night' has slate-coloured rather than green foliage and is now becoming more widely available.

Culture Garden. Both *E. palustris* and *E. gigantea* will grow well in pots or pans placed in a garden pond or in a damp spot in the garden, provided that the rhizomes are above the water level.

Compost C.

Epipactis royleana

Epipactis palustris

Epipactis gigantea, Serpentine Night

GALEARIS

Some ten species, with nine species in China, Korea, eastern Russia and the Himalayas; also a single species in North America.

Recommended The North American *G. spectabilis* and the eastern Asiatic *G. roborowskii*, which has deep purple flowers with a three-lobed lip, not unlike those of *Ponerorochis chusua*.

Habitat Open areas, grassland and open woodland on limestone.

Culture Frost-free greenhouse, seen to their best advantage in pot culture.

Compost B.

Galearis roborowskii

GOODYERA creeping ladies tresses

About 100 species world-wide; a mixture of temperate and tropical species, the latter far outnumbering the former.

Recommended *G. repens*, *G. oblongifolia*, *G. schlechtedahliana*, *G. foliosa*, *G. biflora* and *G. maximowicziana*.

Habitat Most are plants of the floors of coniferous, broadleaf and evergreen forests, where they grow in deep shade.

Culture Frost-free greenhouse. *Goodyera* species are best cultivated in pots or pans placed in shade.

Compost D. Goodyeras can be grown in well-drained composts, such as small-sized pumice, or a mixture of loam, leaf mould and grit.

Goodyera biflora

GYMNADENIA
fragrant orchids

A small genus of perhaps five species from Europe across to the Far East. Some authorities include *Nigritella* and *Leucorchis* within *Gymnadenia* on the basis of DNA evidence.

Recommended The three most common species are the Eurasian *G. conopsea* (our native fragrant orchid), the European *G. odoratissima* (with smaller paler flowers) and *G. orchidis* (a species from the Far East). The fine *G. conopsea* var. *densiflora*, which grows in limestone grassland or, more commonly, in calcareous marshes and fens, flowers a fortnight later than the typical variety and has darker more intensely clove-scented flowers.

Habitat Chalk and limestone grassland, calcareous fens and marshes, woodland margins.

Culture *G. conopsea* can be naturalised or grown on a rock garden in suitable compost. In full sun.

Compost B.

Gymnadenia conopsea var. densiflora

Gymnadenia odoratissima

HABENARIA

Well over 1,000 species with a world-wide distribution, the great majority being found in the tropics and subtropics of both the New and Old Worlds. Most of the hardier species come from the Far East, mostly from Japan, Korea and the mountains of western China.

Recommended *H. radiata*, *H. davidii*, *H. limprichtii* and *H. mairei*.

Habitat Grassland, scrub and open woodland on limestone and other soils, also in seasonally marshy areas. The scarlet-lipped *H. rhodochila* and the flesh-coloured *H. carnea*, both from the Far East, do well in an intermediate glasshouse but are not hardy.

Culture Frost-free greenhouse.

Compost A.

Habenaria radiata

Photo Hiroaki Maeda

HIMANTOGLOSSUM
lizard orchids

Six species in Europe and Mediterranean across to Iran.

Recommended The European *H. hircinum*, *H. adriaticum* (from Italy, the northern Balkans and Hungary), *H. affine* (from Turkey), and *H. caprinum* (from the Balkans, Crete and Turkey).

Habitat Grassland, open areas on limestone, woodland edges, and waste places such as roadside verges.

Culture Frost-free greenhouse, gardens.

Compost A.

Himantoglossum caprinum

LIPARIS

A large predominantly tropical genus, only a few *Liparis* species are hardy.

Recommended The Japanese *L. krameri*, called 'Jigabashisoo' or digger-wasp orchid, because of its dark flowers. *L. makinoana*, 'Suzumushisoo' or singing cricket orchid, also from Japan is similar in its size and habitat preferences.

Habitat Woodland edges and scrub.

Culture Frost-free greenhouse.

Compost D. In pots or pans with a well-drained compost of small-sized pumice or a mixture of loam, grit and leaf mould. The Eurasian *L. loeselii*, a very rare native in the fens of East Anglia and the dune slacks of South Wales, can be cultivated in pots in sphagnum moss if acquired legally.

Liparis loeselii

LISTERA
twayblades

Some 58 species in Europe and Asia. *Listera* has recently been included in the formerly holomycotrophic genus *Neottia* because of DNA-based analyses that have shown that they form a monophyletic clade.

Recommended The Eurasian *L. ovata* sometimes appears spontaneously in gardens, particularly in light woodland or hedgerows. Some of the Asiatic species, although smaller in stature, have larger flowers. A few species, such as *L. puberula*, have leaves that are striped with silvery white.

Habitat In grassy areas, woods and scrub, often on limestone, usually in light shade.

Culture Gardens and frost-free greenhouses.

Compost B.

Listera puberula

NEOFINETIA

Three species from the Far East.

Recommended *N. falcata* (Fruu Ran' in Japanese, meaning noble orchid) received its name because of its association with Ienari Tokugawa (1773–1837), the 11th Shogun, who loved this plant and collected more than 200 varieties of it during his life-time. His feudal lords sought to gain favour by bringing unusual forms to him. It is native to China.

Habitat A woodland lithophyte.

Culture A sunny place in a frost-free greenhouse. *N. falcata* flourishes in places where the temperature stays above 5 °C (41 °F) in winter.

Compost H. *N. falcata* can also be grown on sphagnum moss, tree-fern fibre or other suitable epiphyte composts.

*Neofinetia
falcata,
variegated
leaved form*

*Neofinetia
falcata*

NEOTINEA

Four species in Europe and the Mediterranean.

Recommended The Mediterranean
N. maculata, *N. ustulata* (formerly *Orchis ustulata*), *N. lactea* (*O. lactea*), and *N. tridentata* (*O. tridentata*).

Habitat Grassland and open scrub on limestone.

Culture Frost-free greenhouse, probably best grown in pots.

Compost A.

Neotinea tridentata

Neotinea maculata

NIGRITELLA
vanilla orchids

A small genus of perhaps a dozen closely related species that are confined to the mountains of Europe. These species are distinguished by their non-resupinate red to blackish flowers that smell of vanilla. Recently, DNA-based research has shown the genus to nest in a broadly defined clade that includes *Gymnadenia* (fragrant orchids). They are easily distinguished morphologically by their entire lip, which is uppermost in the flower, and by their fragrance.

Recommended *N. nigra* and *N. rubra*.

Habitat Montane meadows on limestone.

Culture Frost-free greenhouse.

Compost A.

Nigritella nigra

OPHRYS
bee orchids, fly orchids, spider orchids

The genus *Ophrys* is one of the highlights of the European and Mediterranean orchid flora. It is a large genus with a debatable number of species, some claim 250 or more, others fewer than 30. Recent DNA studies indicate that there are relatively few distinct species.

Recommended Several of the showier species do well in cultivation: *O. apifera* (common bee orchid), *O. vernixia* (syn. *O. speculum*) (mirror-of-Venus orchid), *O. lutea* (yellow bee orchid), *O. tenthredinifera*, *O. ferrum-equinum* (horseshoe orchid), *O. bertolonii*, *O. sphegodes* (early spider orchid), *O. mammosa*, *O. fuciflora* (late spider orchid), *O. scolopax* (woodcock orchid) and, two of the best, the Cretan *O. heldreichii* and *O. candica*.

A number of eastern Mediterranean species have a black lip with a bright white speculum. These include *O. kotschyi* from Crete, *O. cilicica* from southern Turkey, *O. cretica* from Crete and the Pelopponese, and *O. reinholdii* from Rhodes and southern Turkey. The hardiest of all is *O. insectifera* (fly orchid).

Habitat Grassland, open areas, open scrub and woodland on the calcareous soils.

Culture *Ophrys* grow well in pans in a frost-free greenhouse.

Compost A. Best re-potted during July or August. Oversized containers can be used so that the plants can be kept in the same pots for several years. *O. apifera* can be naturalised in grassland and often appears on dumped chalk or limestone waste.

Ophrys vernixia

Ophrys kotschyi

Ophrys lutea var. *galilea*

ORCHIS

19 species of Eurasian distribution, extending from the Atlantic seaboard eastward to Lake Baikal and north-western China. A few species are found in Mediterranean North Africa and a solitary species occurs in Madeira.

Recommended *O. purpurea* (lady orchid), *O. simia* (monkey orchid), *O. militaris* (military orchid) and *O. mascula* (early purple orchid).

Hybrids see under *Aceras* (p. 85).

Habitat Grassland, woodland and scrub on limestone or neutral soils.

Culture The larger species can be naturalised in grassland or wild gardens. All grow well in pots or pans in a frost-free greenhouse, although *O. militaris* grows better in a cold frame outside.

Compost B.

Orchis purpurea

PHAIUS

A genus of about 30 species in Asia, Africa, Madagascar and Australasia. Only one or two Asian species are at all hardy.

Recommended The only hardy species is *P. delavayi* (formerly *Calanthe delavayi*) from the high mountains of south-western China.

Habitat In deciduous and mixed woodlands on slopes in shaded places and in rocky stream beds between 2,900 m and 3,300 m elevation.

Culture Rock garden or frost-free greenhouse.

Compost D.

Phaius delavayi

PLATANTHERA

About 85 species with a circumboreal distribution. Superficially, these orchids resemble habenarias but they have very short stigma processes and an entire ligulate or lacerate lip, and the tubers are always digitate.

Recommended

The Eurasian species all have white or greenish flowers with a ligulate unfringed lip, whereas the North American species are often more brightly coloured, even orange- or purple-flowered, and usually have a three-lobed fringed or lacerate lip.

Platanthera chlorantha

Platanthera bifolia

Platanthera japonica

The white-flowered lesser and greater butterfly orchids, respectively *P. bifolia* and *P. chlorantha*, are widespread throughout Europe and temperate Asia. Rather finer is *P. japonica*, a species that is widespread in the Far East.

Among the North American species, the choice species are the greater and lesser purple-fringed orchids, *P. grandiflora* and *P. psycodes*, and the yellow- or orange-flowered *P. ciliaris* (from eastern and southern North America). The white-flowered *P. leucophaea*, also from North America, lacks a fringed lip.

Habitat The Eurasian species grow in woodland, scrub and grassland, often on limestone. The American species grow in slightly acidic swamps, marshes and wet meadows or by streams and rivers in sunny or slightly shaded positions.

Culture The Eurasian species can be naturalised in the garden. The American species are best grown in pots in a frost-free greenhouse.

Compost B.

Platanthera psycodes

Platanthera ciliaris

Platanthera **hybrids**

Pleione forrestii

Pleione formosana

PLEIONE
Nepalese crocus, windowsill orchids

About 22 species in Bhutan, Laos, Myanmar, China, Taiwan, Thailand and Vietnam.

Recommended From the Himalayas, the autumn-flowering *P. praecox* and *P. maculata*, and their natural hybrid *P.* × *lagenaria*, all with two-leaved pseudobulbs, and the rare one-leafed *P. saxicola*. Spring-flowered species are all one-leafed and mostly Chinese: pink- to rose-purple-flowered forms include *P. bulbocodioides*, *P. formosana*, *P. limprichtii*, *P. pleonioides*, *P. yunnanensis* and *P. aurita*; white-flowered forms include *P. grandiflora*, *P. albiflora* and *P. humilis*; and *P. forrestii* has yellow flowers.

Hybrids Large numbers of spectacular hybrids are available. These have longer-lived flowers than the species, are relatively hardy and will survive outside in appropriate conditions. Pink-flowered hybrids include *P.* Versailles and *P.* Teal; *P.* Eiger has white flowers; *P.* Shantung has yellow flowers; *P.* Alishan and *P.* Kilauea have bi-coloured flowers; the flowers of *P.* Rakata and *P.* Zeus Weinstein are pink underlain with yellow; and *P.* Keith Rattray has red flowers.

Pleione bulbocodioides

**Pleione
Santa Maria
'Nightjar'**

Habitat Most hardy species grow in the shade in slightly acidic leaf litter over limestone. Others grow in their natural environments as epiphytes in moss on tree trunks or branches; these include the autumn-flowering species, *P. humilis*, *P. hookeriana*, *P. forrestii* and *P. aurita*.

Culture Frost-free greenhouse in pans. Both *P. limprichtii* and *P. pogonioides* will flourish on a well-drained peat bank outdoors in southern Britain, provided that the pseudobulbs are buried a few centimetres deep in the compost. Dormant pseudobulbs should be stored in a cool, dry place for at least 6–8 weeks if they are to benefit fully from vernalisation. A temperature of 5 °C (41 °F) or less (but not below freezing) is ideal, and can be achieved by placing the pseudobulbs in a garage or outhouse, or in a sealed plastic bag in the bottom of a refrigerator.

Compost E. They should be re-potted annually in the spring, before they come into flower and the new roots begin to emerge.

Pleione grandiflora

**Pleione
Shantung**

POGONIA

Seven species in the Far East and North America.

Recommended *Pogonia japonica*, from China and Japan, where it is called 'Tokisu' or ibis orchid; and the North American *P. ophioglossoides*.

Habitat Grows in damp places and flowers in May and June.

Culture In pots in a frost-free greenhouse.

Compost Well-drained, small-sized pumice is preferred in Japan; it must be kept moist and in a sunny position. The tubers must not be allowed to dry out in the winter.

Pogonia ophioglossoides

Ponerorchis graminifolia

PONERORCHIS

About 15 species, mainly from the alpine areas of eastern Asia, Japan and Taiwan.

Recommended *P. graminifolia* from Japan, China and Taiwan, where its many colour forms are collected with fervour; also the East Asian species *P. chusua*.

Habitat Evergreen forest and meadows in mountainous regions.

Culture Pots in a frost-free greenhouse.

Compost In Japan, *Ponerorchis* species are commonly cultivated in well-drained compost or small-sized pumice and grown in half-shade in summer. The tubers should not be allowed to dry out completely in the winter.

Ponerorchis graminifolia

Ponerorchis graminifolia

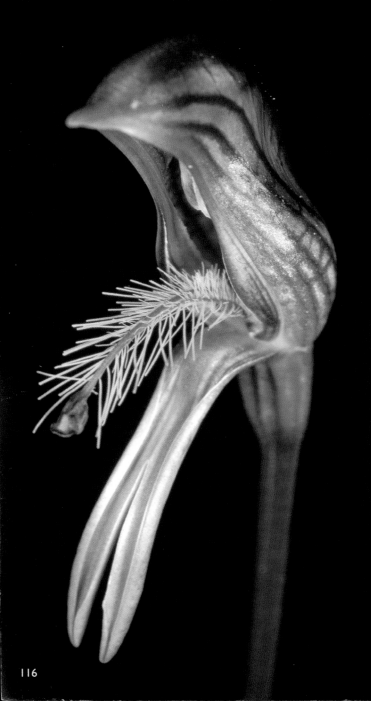

PTEROSTYLIS
greenhoods

About 180 species in Australia with outliers in New Guinea and the adjacent islands, New Caledonia, New Zealand and Ceram.

Recommended The genus can be conveniently divided into three groups: **A.** colony-forming species, **B.** non-colony-forming species, and **C.** the *P. rufa* group and its allies. The colony-forming species are the most rewarding for growers, and include different species that flower in Europe throughout the year. Species that fall into this group are mostly summer- and autumn-flowering and include some with leafy stems, such as *P. concinna, P. laxa, P. pulchella, P. robusta* and *P. truncata*. The winter- or spring-flowering species mostly have basal rosettes of leaves and include *P. baptistii, P. nutans, P. pedunculata, P. concinna, P. curta* and the natural hybrid *P. × ingens*. The latter group are the easier species to cultivate. Species with a feathery lip, such as *P. tasmanica*, do not multiply freely in cultivation.

Habitat Open sandy areas, rocks, scrublands and woodlands on light sandy soils.

Culture Frost-free greenhouse, shaded to 50–70% during summer.

Compost F.

Pterostylis tasmanica

Pterostylis baptistii

SATYRIUM

About 100 species mainly in tropical and subtropical Africa and Madagascar, but the three hardy species are from Asia.

Recommended The closely related *S. ciliatum* and *S. nepalense* have pink flowers and are common in the Himalayas and western China; both flower in the autumn. A third species, the yellow-flowered *S. yunnanense,* is known only from the mountains of south-western China.

Habitat Woodland margins and scrub in shade, up to 3,300 m.

Culture Pots in a frost-free greenhouse.

Compost D.

Satyrium nepalense

SERAPIAS
tongue orchids

About 20 closely allied European and Mediterranean species, which can be difficult to distinguish from each other.

Recommended The most distinctive species is the colony-forming *S. lingua*, which is widespread around the Mediterranean. Larger flowers are found in *S. neglecta, S. orientalis* and *S. vomeracea.*

Habitat Scrub, grassland and waste places, often on the sea-shore.

Culture In pots in a frost-free greenhouse. Possibly hardy in the south of England.

Compost A.

Serapias neglecta

SPIRANTHES
ladies tresses

About 50 species, mainly in North and Central America, with a few species in Europe and a single species in eastern Asia across to Australia.

Recommended The North American *S. cernua* var. *odorata* is white-flowered and sweetly scented. The Far Eastern and Australasian species *S. sinensis* can have pink or white self-pollinating flowers and is a common weed in pots in orchid greenhouses. The diminutive white-flowered European *S. spiralis* (autumn lady's tresses) can be naturalised in lawns on chalky and other limestone substrates; some gardens on the South and North Downs in England support sizeable colonies of this pretty, late-flowering orchid (flowers from August onwards).

Habitat Open grassland, marshes and river-sides.

Culture In pots in a frost-free greenhouse.

Compost B.

Spirathes spiralis

THELYMITRA
sun orchids

Some 80 species from Australia that scarcely look like orchids, having an almost regular brightly coloured flower.

Recommended Amongst the blue-flowered species, *T. crinita, T. ixioides, T. macrophylla* and *T. antennifera* are the easiest to grow. The amazing *T. variegata* (Queen of Sheba orchid) from Western Australia, with its iridescent purple and blue flowers with black spotting, is considered one of Australia's most spectacular species.

Habitat In grassland, scrubs, marshes and sandy acid soils, often in full sun.

Culture Hardy *Thelymitra* species thrive under 50–70% shade cloth in Mediterranean climates, but a heated frame or glasshouse is necessary in colder areas. Light frost to -2 °C (28 °F) does not worry the majority of species. They like good air movement and will not thrive in a stuffy humid atmosphere, especially if temperatures are high.

Compost F. Grow in full sun.

Thelymitra crinata

Thelymitra macrophylla

Thelymitra variegata

Rare hardy species

Calypso bulbosa var. americana

ARETHUSA
dragon's mouth, swamp pink

An American orchid genus of just one species, *Arethusa bulbosa*.

Recommended *A. bulbosa*.

Habitat Acidic sphagnum patches and hummocks within rich grassy fens, peaty meadows.

Culture Cool greenhouse.

Compost G. In full sun.

CALYPSO

Monotypic, circumboreal.

Recommended *C. bulbosa* has four varieties: var. *bulbosa* from northern Europe and Asia, var. *occidentalis* from Alaska, British Colombia and adjacent Oregon and Idaho, var. *americana* from north-eastern and north-central North America, and var. *speciosa* from Japan, Korea and China.

Habitat In coniferous woods and on mounds in sphagnum bogs and marshes.

Culture Cool greenhouse.

Compost G. *C. bulbosa* can be very difficult to keep alive for more than a year.

CHANGNIENIA

Monotypic and endemic to central China.

Recommended

C. amoena.

Habitat

In shady places in open forest, in humus-rich soils at elevations up to 1,800 m.

Culture Garden, cool greenhouse.

Compost C.

Changnienia amoena

COMPERIA

A monotypic genus from some of the larger islands off the west coast of Turkey, mainland Anatolia, the Crimea and across to northern Iran.

Comperia comperiana

Recommended
C. comperiana.

Habitat Sandy calcareous soils in grassland and light woodland, usually in sunny or half-shade positions.

Culture Frost-free glasshouse, in sheltered spot in the garden.

Compost A.

CREMASTRA

Three species from the Far East.

Recommended
C. appendiculata from China, Korea, Japan and the Himalayas.

Habitat Woodlands, in shade.

Culture Cool greenhouse.

Compost D. In shade.

Cremastra appendiculata

Orchid language

agar: a gelatinous polysaccharide extracted from red algae that is commonly used as a setting agent in microbiology and tissue culture. For most purposes, 6–8 g of agar per litre of culture medium will produce a suitably solid gel.

anther: the male, pollen bearing, part of the flower.

asymbiotic: in the context of orchid seed germination, this means without the aid of a compatible fungus.

calcifuge: a plant that dislikes alkaline soils.

calyx: the outer whorl of floral segments. Each part of the calyx is called a sepal. The calyx usually protects the bud before the flower opens.

capsule: botanically speaking, the correct term for a seed 'pod'.

CBD: The Convention on Biological Diversity. An international convention that confirms national ownership of biological materials and controls access to germplasm.

chlorosis: a yellowing of the foliage.

CITES: International Convention in Trade in Endangered Species of Fauna and Flora. An international convention that controls trade in endangered and threatened plants and animals.

climax vegetation: a community of plants that has reached a steady state through the process of ecological succession. This equilibrium occurs because the climax community is composed of species best adapted to average conditions in the area.

clone: one of two or more of genetically identical individuals.

column: the central structure in the orchid flower, derived from a combination of the male and female parts of the flower.

corolla: the second whorl of segments of the flower, each part being called a petal.

cotyledon: a seedling leaf.

culture medium: any combination of ingredients suitable for the culture of orchid seed or seedlings.

desiccant: any substance that will absorb moisture. In addition to the commonly used chemical desiccants, dried rice is a useful desiccant, but it must be dried in an oven at 105 °C (221 °F) for at least 3 hours before use and it must be regenerated regularly.

diploid: possessing two chromosome sets.

distilled water: water free of any dissolved mineral salts. This can be produced by boiling water and collecting the condensate.

ecological succession: the development of the vegetation in an area over time.

embryo: the part of the seed that develops into a plant.

epiphyte: A plant that grows upon another plant (such as a tree) non-parasitically or sometimes upon some other object (such as a building or a telegraph wire). These plants derive their moisture and nutrients from the air and rain and sometimes from debris that accumulates around them.

hermetically sealed: sealed so that moisture can neither enter nor escape. Ideally, seed should be stored in a hermetically sealed container to maintain a constant seed moisture content.

hypha (plural **hyphae**): a long, branching filamentous thread-like structure of a fungus. The threads are often woven into a mat-like structure in the soil, which is called the mycelium.

inorganic: compounds that do not contain carbon.

ion: a charged particle. Calcium phosphate, for example, breaks down in solution into calcium ions and phosphate ions.

in vitro: literally meaning 'in glass', referring to the culture of plant material in glass vessels such as Petri dishes, test-tubes, flasks or jars.

in vivo: in a living state, refers to plants growing in nature or outside the laboratory.

Kilner jar: a preserving jar with a natural rubber seal. Such jars form an effective and long-lasting seal as long as the seals are renewed on a ten-year cycle.

labellum: alternative term for the lip of an orchid.

lip: a highly modified petal that acts as a flag to attract pollinators and often acts as a landing platform. In slipper orchids, the lip modified to form a pouch that traps potential insect pollinators.

lithophyte: a plant that grows in or on rocks.

mycorrhiza: a symbiotic (generally mutualistic, but occasionally weakly pathogenic) association between a fungus and the roots of a vascular plant. In a mycorrhizal association, the fungus colonises the host plants' roots, either intracellularly, as in arbuscular mycorrhizal fungi, or extracellularly, as in ectomycorrhizal fungi.

organic: containing carbon (excluding carbon dioxide).

ovary: the structure that contains the ovules and develops into the seed capsule. In orchids, the ovary is found immediately behind the flower.

ovule: female gamete (reproductive cell) or egg.

parasite: an organism that harms another.

peloton: fungal hyphal coils within host plant cells.

pH: a measure of the degree of acidity or alkalinity of a solution. The pH scale goes from zero to 14. pH 7 is neutral. Figures below pH 7 indicate progressively more acid solutions; figures above pH 7 indicate increasingly more alkaline solutions.

Petri dish: a shallow dish with an overlapping lid developed by the German bacteriologist R. J. Petri. Both glass and sterile disposable plastic Petri dishes can be purchased in bulk.

Perlite: an amorphous volcanic glass that has a relatively high water content. Perlite can be used as a soil amendment that helps to prevent water loss and soil compaction.

plate: often used to mean a Petri dish.

pollen: male gamete (reproductive cell).

pollinium (plural pollinia): in orchids, the pollen grains are aggregated into masses, which may be sticky (as in slipper orchids) or hard.

protocorm: instead of producing roots and shoots, germinating orchid seeds develop into a ball of cells called a protocorm.

rhizoid: similar in appearance to a root hair.

rhizome: a horizontal underground stem.

rostellum: a flap of tissue that separates the anther and the stigma. The portion of the stigma that assists in gluing of the pollinia to the pollinator.

salep: Dried and ground wild-collected tubers of selected European orchids, forming a powder that is used as a pick-me-up or aphrodisiac, mainly in Turkey and Greece.

sepal: one of the outer three floral segments. In other plant families, sepals are often green and scale-like, whereas in the Orchidaceae, they are often of a colour similar to that of the petals.

Seramis®: granules made from pure mined clay that is liquefied, porosised, dried, broken up and fired. The water-retention features of this product allow each granule to store more than 100% of its weight in water, while at the same time draining any excess.

silica gel: a commonly used desiccant that can inadvertently lead to over-drying of seed and loss of viability. Sachets of silica gel that contain a moisture-level indicator are, however, valuable for monitoring the potential leakage of moisture from the atmosphere into sealed vessels.

staminode: a structure found in the centre of the flowers of slipper orchids that often hides the pollen and the stigma.

stratification: pre-treatment of seeds by simulating winter conditions so that germination can occur.

summer green: bearing leaves throughout the summer months.

symbiosis: a mutually beneficial relationship.

synsepal: flower part formed by the fusion of the two lower sepals of a slipper orchid.

testa: the seed coat that surrounds the embryo.

tuber: a swollen root. Strictly speaking, orchid tubers are tuberoids, formed from the base of the stem.

vernalisation: the acquisition of a plant's ability to flower or germinate in the spring by exposure to the prolonged cold of winter.

winter-green: producing leaves over the winter months rather than in the summer.

Want to know more?

Read about hardy orchids

Bailes, C. (2005). Hardy exotics and native beauties. *The Garden* 130: 342–347.

Cribb, P. J. & Bailes, C. (1989). *Hardy Orchids*. Croom Helm, London.

Cribb, P. J. & Butterfield, I. (1999). *The Genus* Pleione. 2nd ed. Royal Botanic Gardens, Kew.

Dash, A. (1999). Dactylorhizas from seed. *The Hardy Orchid Society Newsletter* 12: 14–18.

Jones, D. L. & Clements, M. A. (2002). A new classification of *Pterostylis* R. Br. (Orchidaceae). *Australian Orchid Research* 4: 64–124.

McKendrick, S. L. (1995). The effects of herbivory and vegetation on laboratory raised *Dactylorhiza praetermissa* (orchidaceae) planted into grassland in southern England. *Biological Conservation* 73: 215–220.

Malmgren, S. (1992). Large scale asymbiotic propagation of *Cypripedium calceolus* — plant physiology from a surgeon's point of view. *Botanic Gardens Micropropagation News* 1: 59–63.

Malmgren, S. (2002). Growing *Ophrys* downstairs. *The Hardy Orchid Society Newsletter* 24: 15–18.

Maunder, M. (1992) Plant reintroduction: an overview. *Biodiversity & Conservation* 1: 51–61.

Lang, D. (2004). *Britain's Orchids*. Wild Guides, Maidenhead, UK.

Light, M. H. S. (1992). Raising pleiones from seed. *Orchid Review* 100: 7–10.

Richards, H., Wootton, R. & Datodi, R. (1988). *Cultivation of Australian Native Orchids*, 2nd ed. Australasian Native Orchid Society Victorian Group Inc., Melbourne.

Ramsay, M. M. & Dixon, K. W. (2003). Propagation science, recovery and translocation of terrestrial orchids. In Dixon, K. W., Kell, S. P., Barrett, R. L. & Cribb, P. J., eds, *Orchid Conservation*. Natural History Publications, Kota Kinabalu, Sabah. pp. 259–288.

Seaton, P. T. & Ramsay, M. M. (2005). *Growing Orchids from Seed*. Royal Botanic Gardens, Kew, Richmond, UK.

Swarts, N. D. & Dixon, K. W. (2009). Terrestrial orchid conservation in the age of extinction. *Annals of Botany* 104: 543–556.

Turner Ettlinger, D. M. (1997). *Notes on British and Irish Orchids*. D. M. Turner Ettlinger, Dorking, UK.

Interesting websites

Forum "Cypripedium". www.cypripedium.de/forum

Frosch's Cypripedium Infos. www.w-frosch.de/

The Slipper Orchid Forum. www.slipperorchidforum.com

Orchid Propagation by Svante Malmgren and Henric Nyström. www.lidaforsgarden.com/orchids

Australia's Native Orchids by Les Nesbitt. http://asgap.org.au/APOL19/sep00-1.html.

Index

Images indicated by bold numbers

A

Aceras 85, 109
   A. anthropophorum **85**
Amitostigma 85
   A. lepidum 85
   A. monanthum **85**
   A. tibeticum 85
Anacamptis 21, 86
   A. coriophora 86
   A. laxiflora 86
   A. morio **8**, **17**, **86**
   A. papilionaceae **10**, 86
   A. pyramidalis **19**, **41**, 86
anther 10
ants **44**, 46
aphids 46
Arethusa 27, 121
   A. bulbosa, 121

B

Barlia 86
   B. metlesicsiana 86
   B. robertiana **86**
bees, as pests 47
Bletilla 18, 26, 87
   B. formosana 87
   B. ochracea 87
   B. striata **3**, 87
   B. Brigantes 87
   B. Coritani 87
   B. Yokohama 87
bog gardens **38**, 39
buying plants 23

C

Caladenia 88
   C. cairnsiata 88
   C. carnea 88
   C. catenata 88
   C. deformis (now Cyanicula
      deformis) **88**
   C. dilatata 88
   C. flava **88**
   C. gemmata (now Cyanicula
      gemmata) 88

   C. latifolia 88
   C. menziesii 88
   C. patersonii 88
Calanthe 18, 26, 89
   C. aristulifera 89
   C. delavayi (now Phaius delavayi) **109**
   C. discolor 89
   C. gracilflora 89
   C. hancockii **8**
   C. izu-insularis **89**
   C. sieboldii 89
   C. striata **89**
   C. tricarinata **89**
   C. Satsuma 89
   C. Takane 89
Calopogon 27, 90
   C. pulchellus 90
   C. tuberosus **90**
Calypso 27, 121
   C. bulbosa 121
      var. americana **121**
      var. occidentalis 121
      var. speciosa **17**, 121
capsules 12, **58**
Cephalanthera 26, 90
   C. damasonium 90
   C. falcata 90
   C. longifolia **18**, **90**
   C. rubra 90
chalk 17
Changnienia 121
   C. amoena **121**
Chloraea **12**, 27, 91
   C. bletioides **91**
   C. chrysantha 91
   C. crispa 91
   C. cylindrostachya 91
   C. gavilu 91
   C. incisa 91
   C. lechleri 91
   C. leptopetala 91
   C. magellanica 91
   C. virescens **91**
climate 17, 18
Coeloglossum 92
   C. viride **92**
collection from the wild 21, 22
column **9**, 10, 11
companion plants 43

Comperia 121
   C. comperiana **121**
competition 19
composts 24–27, 32, 33
conservation 21– 23
Corybas 92
   C. aconitiflorus 92
   C. diemenicus 92
   C. fimbriatus 92
   C. hispidus 92
   C. incurvus 92
   C. orbicularis **92**
   C. pruinosus 92
Cremastra 121
   C. appendiculata **121**
Cymbidium **7**, 26, 93
   C. ensifolium **93**
   C. faberi 93
   C. goeringii **8**, **93**
   C. kanran 93
   C. sinense 93
   C.× ventricosum 95
Cypripedium 10, 11, **13**, 14, 18, 21,
   26, 30, 35, 72–79, 94
   in the garden 79
   in the greenhouse 52, **78**
   life cycle 73
   hybrids **5**, **43**, **95**
   potting on 32
   raising seedlings 55
   re-potting **34**
   seed **53**
      germination **74**–76
      sterilisation 75
   transplanting protocorms of 77
   C. acaule **17**, 95
   C. arietinum 94
   C. calceolus **19**, **20**, **21**, **75**, **77**,
      94, 95
   C. calcicola 94
   C. californicum **94**
   C. candidum 94
   C. debile 94
   C. fargesii 94
   C. farreri 94
   C. fasciolatum 94, **95**
   C. flavum 94, 95
   C. formosanum **94**
   C. franchetii 94

   C. guttatum 73, **94**
   C. henryi 94, 95
   C. japonicum 94
   C. kentuckiense **18**, 94, 95
   C. lentiginosum 94
   C. lichiangense 94
   C. macranthos **20**, **50**, 73, 94, 95
   C. margaritaceum **8**, 94
   C. montanum 94
   C. palangshanensene 94
   C. parviflorum 94, 95
      var. pubescens **79**, **94**, 95
   C. plectrochilum 74, 94
   C. reginae 94, 95
   C. segawai 94
   C. tibeticum **6**, 94
   C. yunnanense **76**, 94
   C. Emil 95
   C. Hank Small 95
   C. Inge 95
   C. Lucy Pinkepank **72**
   C. Michael 95
   C. Philipp 95
   C. Sabine 95
   C. Ulla Silkens 95
   C. Victoria 95
Cryptolaemus montrouzieri **45**

D

Dactylorhiza 15, 29, **30**, 33, 35, **37**,
   56–63, 92, 96
   capsules 58
   during the summertime 63
   life cycle of 56, 57
   overwintering 62
   potting on 32, 62
   raising seedlings 55, 58–61
   re-potting **35**
   seed germination 58, 59
   D. aristata 96
   D. elata **56**, **96**
   D. foliosa **5**, **96**
   D. fuchsii **40**, **41**, **56**, **61**, 96
   D. maculata **13**, 17, **38**, **62**, **63**, 96
   D. praetermissa **41**, **59**, 96
   D. purpurella 96
   D. romana 15
   D. sambucina **19**, 96
   D. × grandis **42**, 96

Dactylostalix 97
   D. ringens 97
de-flasking 30, 31
Dendrobium 27, 97
   D. moniliforme 97
Disa 27, 98
   D. aurata **98**
   D. cardinalis 98
   D. tripetaloides 98
   D. uniflora **98**
   D. Kewensis 98
   D. Kirstenbosch Pride 98
   D. Watsonii 98
disease 23, 33, 37
Diuris 99
   D. behrii 99
   D. corymbosa 99
   D. fragantissima **99**
   D. longifolia 99
   D. maculata 99
   D. magnifica 99
   D. pardina **99**
   D. punctata 99
   D. sulphurea 99
dormancy 51
   cold-induced 51
   drought-induced 51
drainage 17, 32, 33, 37

E
endosperm 9
Epipactis 26, 29, 37, 100
   E. gigantea 29, **100**
   E. helleborine 100
   E. mairei **8**, 100
   E. palustris **100**
   E. royleana **100**
   E. thunbergii 100
   E. veratrifolia 100
   E. xanthophaea 100
   E. aphyllum 14
   E. Sabine **37**, 100

F
false spider mites 47
fertilisers 10, 21, 26, 34
flower structure 9, 10, **11**
fungal association **9**, **14**, 17, 19, 34, 37

G
Galearis 101
   G. roborowskii **84**, **101**
   G. spectabilis 101
germination 9, 14, 15, 54
   asymbiotic **60**, 66, 74–76
   symbiotic **59**, 67, 77
Goodyera 101
   G. biflora **101**
   G. foliosa 101
   G. maximowicziana 101
   G. oblongifolia 101
   G. repens 101
   G. schlechtedahliana 101
growth medium 14
Gymnadenia 102, 107
   G. conopsea 102
      var. *densiflora* **102**
   G. odoratissima **102**
   G. orchidis 102

H
Habenaria 103
   H. carnea 103
   H. davidii 103
   H. limprichtii 103
   H. mairei 103
   H. radiata **103**
   H. rhodochila 103
habitat 17
   fragmentation of 21
Hammarbya paludosa 17
hardy orchid societies 22, 52, 58
herbaceous borders 39
Himantoglossum 86, 103
   H. adriaticum 103
   H. affine 103
   H. caprinum **103**
   H. hircinum **8**, 103
humidity 33
hybrids 5, 23, 38

L
leaves, 13
legal protection 22
Leuchorchis 102
limestone 17
lip 10, 11
Liparis 104
   L. krameri 104

L. loeselii 17, 104
L. makinosana 104
Listera 104
   L. ovata 104
   L. puberula **104**
living roofs 39

M
mealy bugs 45, 47
Mediterranean environment 7
Microtis media 19
mowing 37, 40, 42, 43
mycorrhiza 9, **14**

N
naturalisation 41
nectar 10
Neofinetia 27, 105
   N. falcata **105**
Neotinea 14, 106
   N. lactea 106
   N. maculata **106**
   N. tridentata **106**
   N. ustulata 106
Neottia 104
   N. nidus-avis 14, **15**
Nigritella 102, 107
   N. nigra **107**
   N. rubra 107
nutrient deficiencies 23
nutrients 14, 17, 34

O
Ophrys 7, 11, 14, 29, 30, 31, 64–71, 108
   germination 66, 67
   life cycle 64, 65
   overwintering 70
      potting on 33, 69, 70
      raising seedlings 55, 66–68
      re-potting **35**
      summer dormancy 71
   O. apifera 10, 11, 19, **31**, 64, **65**, **66**, **67**, 108
   O. bertolonii 108
   O. candica 108
   O. cilicica 108
   O. cretica 108
   O. ferrum-equinum 108
   O. fusca **70**
   O. fusiflora **64**, 108

O. heldreichii 108
O. insectifera 108
O. kotschyi **108**
O. lutea **17**, 108
   var. *galilea* **108**
O. mammosa **8**, 108
O. reinholdii 108
O. scolopax 108
O. speculum (now *O. vernixia*) **108**
O. sphegodes **22**, 108
O. tenthredinifera **4**, **39**, 108
O. vernixia 108
Orchiaceras × *bergonii* 85
Orchiaceras × *duhartii* 85
Orchiaceras × *spuria* 85
Orchis 14, 21, 29, 31, 85, 86, 109
   O. anatolica 15
   O. lactea (now *Neotinea lactea*) 106
   O. italica **31**
   O. mascula 109
   O. militaris 85, 109
   O. pauciflora 15
   O. purpurea 85, **109**
   O. quadripunctata 15
   O. simia 85, 109
   O. tridentata (now
      Neotinea tridentata) 106
   O. ustulata (now *Neotinea ustulata*)
      106
ovary 10

P
pests 45–49
   biological control of 45, 47, 48, 49
   chemical control of 45, 47
petals 10, 11
Phaius 109
   P. delavayi **109**
pioneer plants 19
planting out 37
Platanthera 110
   P. bifolia **110**, 111
   P. chlorantha **110**, 111
   P. ciliaris **111**
   P. grandiflora 111
   P. japonica **110**, 111
   P. leucophaea 111
   P. psycodes **111**
Pleione 7, 11, 26, 29, 47, 112

bulb **7**
during the summertime 83
feeding 83
hybrids **23**,113
life cycle 80, 81
overwintering 82
re-potting 82
P. albiflora 112
P. aurita 22,112, 113
P. bulbocodioides **112**
P. formosana **16, 112**
P. forrestii **112**, 113
P. grandiflora 112, **113**
P. hookeriana 113
P. humilis 112, 113
P. limprichtii **36**, 112, 113
P. maculata 83, 112
P. plenioides 112
P. pogonioides 113
P. praecox **83**, 112
P. saxicola 112
P. yunnanensis 112
P. × lagenaria 112
P. Bonobo **28**
P. Santa Maria 'Nightjar' **113**
P. Shantung **113**
P. Versailles **80**, 112
plunge beds 32, 33
Pogonia 114
    P. japonica 114
    P. ophioglossoides **114**
pollen 10, 11
pollination 10, 11, 12
    artificial 11, 43
pollinia 10, 11, **12**
Ponerorchis 101, 115
    P. chusua 115
    P. graminifolia **115**
pots 32
potting on 30–33
propagation 22, 29, 52–55
    from seed 22, 52–55
    vegetative 29
protocorm **9**, **14**, **59**, 68
pseudobulb 7, 29, 81
Pterostylis 116
    P. baptistii **116**
    P. concinna 116

P. curta 116
P. laxa 116
P. nutans 116
P. pedunculata 116
P. pulchella 116
P. robusta 116
P. rufa 116
P. tasmanica **116**
P. truncata 116
P. × ingens 11

R
rainfall 17, 18
raised beds 37
red spider mites, 48
re-potting **34, 35**, 47
reproductive organs **10**
resupination 10
Rhinanthus sp. **41**
rhizome 7
root **9**, 14, 35
rosette **7**
Royal Botanic Gardens, Kew 3, 21, 42
S
Sainsbury Orchid Conservation
    Project 3
Satyrium 117
    S. ciliatum 117
    S. nepalense **117**
    S. yunnanense 117
scale insects 48
scented 38
seed **9, 12, 14**, 19, **59**
    coat 9, **12**
    dormancy 15
    sterilisation 75
    obtaining 53
    quality 53
    storage 53
seed bank 22
seedlings, 30, 31, 54,55
    care of 54, 55
    weaning of 30, 31
self-pollination 10
sepals 10, 11
Serapias 29, 31, 117
    S. lingua 29, 117
    S. neglecta **117**
    S. olbia 29

S. orientalis 117
S. vomeracea 117
shade 17, 18, 39
slugs 32, 37, 45, 49
snails 37, 45, 49
soil 17, 37
    pH 17, 27, 37
    structure 17
    maintaining low nutrient status
        of 37
Spiranthes 18, 118
    S. cernua 17
        var. *odorata* 118
    S. sinensis 118
    S. spiralis **118**
stigma 10
substrate 14, 17
summer dormancy 29, 31
summer-green species 29, 30, 35
temperature 17, 18, 27
T
Thelymitra 119
    T. antennifera 119
    T. crinata **119**
    T. ixioides 119
    T. macrophylla **119**
    T. variegata **119**
threatened orchids 21
Tortrix moth caterpillars 49
trap flowers 10
tubers 7, 21, 29, 31
V
vanilla orchids 107
Vanilla planifolia **13**
velamen 7, **9**
vernalisation 15, 30, 77
viruses 49
W
watering 17, 32, 37, 82
weaning 30, 31
windowsill orchids 112
winter-green species 7, 26, 30, 31,
    34
woodlice 49
Y
yellow rattle **41**

autumn lady's tresses 118
bee orchid 11, 19, 64, 65, 108
bee orchid family 108
bird's nest orchid 14, **15**
bog orchid 17
British ghost orchid 14
broad-leaved helleborine 100
bug orchid 86
butterfly orchid 86
common spotted orchid **41, 57**
creeping ladies tresses 101
digger-wasp orchid 104
donkey orchids 99
dragon's mouth 121
early purple orchid 109
fly orchid 108
fragrant orchids 102, 107
frog orchids 92
giant orchid 86
grass pink 90
greater purple-fringed orchid 111
greenhoods 116
green-winged orchid 86
hardy slipper orchids 94
heath spotted orchid 96
helleborine orchids 90, 100
helmet orchids 92
horseshoe orchid 108
hyacinth orchid 87
ladies tresses 118
lady orchid 109
lady's slipper orchids 21, 94
late spider orchid 108
lax-flowered orchid 86
lesser purple-fringed orchid **111**
lizard orchids 103
man orchid **85**
marsh helleborine 100
marsh orchids 96
military orchid 109
mirror-of-Venus orchid **108**
moccasin orchid 79
monkey orchid 109
nepalese crocus 112
noble orchid **105**
pyramidal orchid 86
Queen of Sheba orchid 119
ram's head slipper orchids 94
singing cricket orchid 104
spider orchids 88, 108
spotted orchids 96
swamp pink 121
tongue orchids 117
woodcock orchid 108
yellow bee orchid **108**

Acknowledgements

Between them, the authors have considerable experience with hardy orchids ranging from taxonomy, field studies and practical conservation through to the germination of seed and cultivation in pots and in the garden. It hardly seems possible, however, for any one person to possess the required expertise in all areas. Where our knowledge has been lacking, we have consulted a wide range of publications and growers and we are grateful for their advice, which was always freely given. There is a wide range of opinions on how to grow hardy orchids from seed and there is certainly no unique answer for any individual species. The experience of individual growers has usually been hard-won over many years of successes and failures. We hope that this book goes some way towards reflecting the differing views within the orchid community. Orchid growers are generous people, and this book could not have been written without the participation of many experienced and not-so-experienced growers. We would particularly like to express our heartfelt thanks to Svante Malmgren, Yu Zhang (Beijing Botanical Gardens), Holger Perner, Matt Richards (Atlanta Botanical Garden), Ian Butterfield, Werner Frosch, Richard Manuel, Johan Blatter, Barry Tattershall and Patricio Novoa (National Botanic Garden, Viña del Mar, Chile). However, the opinions expressed in this book are the sole responsibility of the authors.

We would like to thank the following for permission to use their photographs: Dana Christen, Joan Cooper, Richard Evenden, Werner Frosch, Lauren Gardiner, Paul Harcourt Davies, Harry Jans, Danny Lentz, Paul Little, Carlyle Luer, Andrew McRobb, Patricio Novoa, Holger Perner, Matt Richards, Maarten Sepp (p.8 *O. mammosa*), Samuel Springer, Maren Talbot, the late Derek Turner Ettlinger, Zhangfenyao and others as cited.